The Digital Reconstruction of Healthcare

Transitioning from Brick and Mortar to Virtual Care

T0132558

The Digital Reconstruction of Healthcare

Transitioning from Brick and Mortar to Virtual Care

Paul Cerrato and **John Halamka**

CRC Press
Taylor & Francis Group
Boca Raton London New York

CRC Press is an imprint of the
Taylor & Francis Group, an **informa** business

First Edition published 2021

by CRC Press
6000 Broken Sound Parkway NW, Suite 300, Boca Raton, FL 33487-2742

and by CRC Press
2 Park Square, Milton Park, Abingdon, Oxon, OX14 4RN

ISBN: 978-1-032-01513-2 (hbk)
ISBN: 978-0-367-55597-9 (pbk)
ISBN: 978-1-003-09423-4 (ebk)

There are rare moments in history when technology, policy, and urgency to change converge. This is one of those moments.

Contents

Preface

When Technology, Policy, and the Urgency to Change Converge

In our last 2 books, we began the conversation discussing the power of words, including misdiagnosis, cynicism, and optimism.[1,2] In this book, our focus is on *reconstruction*, and all its implications for healthcare. To some, it might suggest the tearing down of an existing structure, a complete replacement of the healthcare ecosystem as we know it. Neither of us believe that's warranted. Our goal, instead, is to address the unsustainable situation that we currently face in the United States and around the globe, and the emerging digital tools that are transforming patient care.

These solutions are not intended to demolish the foundation upon which medicine is built, but neither are they designed to patch up crumbling walls or apply duct tape to the ineffective, cost-prohibitive practices currently in place. To extend the metaphor: The foundation of healthcare may remain solid, but many of the walls, floors, windows, and doors that sit on this foundation are rotting and need to be replaced. The next 8 chapters will provide evidence from multiple sources, including deep learning specialists, consultations with thought leaders and government officials around the world, peer-reviewed studies, unpublished data, and cutting-edge initiatives at Mayo Clinic and several other healthcare leaders—in addition to our combined 60+ years of experience working in healthcare. The preponderance of evidence from all these sources makes a compelling argument: Business as usual is no longer an option; the digital reconstruction of healthcare is no longer on the world's wish list. It's becoming a sustainable reality—and one that is all the more necessary in light of the COVID-19 pandemic. That reality will include the partial shift from caring for patients in hospitals, clinics, and medical offices to meeting their needs through telemedicine, hospital-at-home programs, and remote patient monitoring.

In Chapter 1, we address the question: Is digital reconstruction necessary? and include a review of the evidence on the effectiveness of digital healthcare, the shortcomings of episodic patient care, diagnostic errors, and our inadequate infrastructure.

Chapter 2 looks at the merits and limitations of telemedicine, hospital and home, and remote patient monitoring. It offers advice on making informed telemedicine choices and the impact of COVID-19, and provides a review of the scientific evidence. We also take a closer look at Mayo Clinic's Advanced Care at Home program.

Chapter 3 discusses the digital assault on COVID-19, including the development of better predictive and diagnostic tools, expanding the knowledge base to address the pandemic, and the importance of taking a holistic approach to the infection.

Chapter 4 once again explores the value of big data, artificial intelligence (AI), and machine learning (ML), a topic we have looked at in several previous books. The discussion analyzes the evidence in diabetes, cardiovascular disease, cancer, gastroenterology, and psychiatry. We also address one of the most difficult issues in medicine: When does correlation imply causality? Finally, we devote a section to advanced data analytics, including summary of how Mayo Clinic's Clinical Data Analytics Platform operates.

Chapter 5, Exploring the Artificial Intelligence/Machine Learning Toolbox, is a primer on artificial neural networks, random forest modeling, gradient boosting, clustering, and linear and logistic regression. We are working from the assumption that many readers do not have a background in statistics or data science and hope these brief tutorials translate these complex topics into plain English.

Chapter 6 dives into the many conversational technologies emerging in healthcare. We begin with the role of natural language processing and then discuss the potential of voice technology to help diagnose disease and the role of Siri, Google Assistant, Alexa, and other patient-facing tools. Finally, we emphasize the urgent need to fight misinformation—with truth and trust.

Chapter 7, Securing the Future of Digital Health, tackles one of healthcare's most vexing problems: cyberattacks. We outline the need for comprehensive risk analysis and staff education to reduce the risk of phishing attacks, along with several basic precautionary steps, including encryption, strong passwords, firewalls, and the like. We also include a section on one of the most vulnerable parts of the healthcare ecosystem: the Internet of Medical Things.

Finally, in Chapter 8, we explore international initiatives to digitally reconstruct healthcare. Specific programs in the United Kingdom, China, and the Netherlands are discussed, as are the needs of low-resource nations.

The emergence of the numerous digital health solutions discussed in the following pages does not imply that information technology will singlehandedly rebuild the healthcare ecosystem. Healthcare needs much more than that. Call it "intensive lifestyle management." Unfortunately, too many IT enthusiasts see technology as a savior and are eager to invest billions of dollars in setting up countless initiatives, platforms, and networks in the hope that they will create a more cost-effective system. That kind of magical thinking is doomed to failure over the long term. If properly deployed, technology will *augment* other resources much like AI-fueled algorithms are now augmenting the diagnosis of eye disease and cancer. Society will still need to address the underlying cultural, financial, and clinical root causes behind our failing healthcare system—issues that are beyond the scope of this book. We both have the humility to recognize that digital health, and all the tools it brings to bear, are only part of the solution. Our experience and research, nonetheless, demonstrate that they are a crucial part of that solution.

— Paul Cerrato, MA
— John Halamka, MD, MS

References

1. Cerrato P, Halamka J. *Reinventing Clinical Decision Support: Data Analytics. Artificial Intelligence, and Diagnostic Reasoning.* Boca Raton, FL: CRC Press/Taylor & Francis Group; 2020.
2. Cerrato P, Halamka J. *The Transformative Power of Mobile Medicine: Leveraging Innovation, Seizing Opportunities, and Overcoming Obstacles of mHealth.* Cambridge, MA: Academic Press/Elsevier; 2019.

Acknowledgments

We want to thank the remarkable Mayo Clinic Platform team, who are reimagining the future of healthcare through digital technology, and Gianrico Farrugia, MD, president and CEO of Mayo Clinic, for recognizing the power of platforms in healthcare.

About the Authors

Paul Cerrato, MA, is the senior research analyst and communications specialist for the Mayo Clinic Platform, which includes three sub-platforms that focus on clinical data analytics, remote diagnostics and management, and virtual health services, including Advanced Care at Home and telemedicine. Mr. Cerrato has more than 35 years of experience working in healthcare as a medical journalist, research analyst, clinician, and educator. He has served as the Editor of *InformationWeek Healthcare*; Executive Editor of *Contemporary OB/GYN*; Senior Editor of *RN Magazine*; and contributing writer/editor for the Yale University School of Medicine, the American Academy of Pediatrics, InformationWeek, Medscape, and MedpageToday. The Health Information Management Systems Society (HIMSS) has listed Mr. Cerrato as one of the most influential healthcare IT columnists. Among his achievements are six editorial awards from the American Business Media—often referred to as the Pulitzer Prize of business journalism—and the Gold Award from the American Society of Healthcare Publications Editors for best-signed editorial.

John D. Halamka, MD, MS, president of the Mayo Clinic Platform, leads a portfolio of platform businesses focused on transforming healthcare by leveraging artificial intelligence, connected healthcare devices, and a network of trusted partners. Trained in emergency medicine and medical informatics, Dr. Halamka has been developing and implementing healthcare information strategy and policy for more than 25 years.

Prior to his appointment at Mayo Clinic, Dr. Halamka was chief information officer at Beth Israel Deaconess Medical Center and Harvard Medical School. He is a practicing emergency medicine physician. As the International Healthcare Innovation Professor at Harvard Medical School, Dr. Halamka helped the George W. Bush administration, the Obama administration, and governments around the world plan their healthcare information strategies. A member of the National Academy of Medicine, Dr. Halamka has written a dozen books about technology-related issues, hundreds of articles, and thousands of posts on the Geekdoctor blog.

He also runs Unity Farm Sanctuary in Sherborn, Massachusetts—the largest animal sanctuary in New England.

Chapter 1

Is Digital Reconstruction Necessary?

In the United States, healthcare spending increased from \$74.6 billion in 1970 to \$3.5 trillion in 2017. Most health economists agree that this steep climb in expenditures is unsustainable.[1] As we write this chapter, projections for 2020 are not very encouraging: PwC's Health Research Institute anticipates a 5% net growth increase in medical costs for 2020.[2] One would expect exceptional quality of care at this price, but the US healthcare system ranks last among 11 high-income countries, with higher morbidity and mortality rates for preventable disorders.[3] The causes of this disparity between costs and quality of care would require an in-depth analysis that is beyond the scope of this book. Our primary goal here is to explore the role of information technology (IT) and the possible impact that digital solutions may have on this health crisis.

In this context, it is instructive to review one of the potential solutions discussed in the PwC report: "Employers and payers will nudge people toward lower-cost sites of care. Payers are designing plans to encourage members to choose free-standing facilities and in-home care, rather than more expensive sites. How those benefits are designed and how employees perceive the costs will shape the effectiveness of site of care strategies. Payers and employers are aiming to grow the role of telemedicine as employees grow more comfortable with it, especially if out-of-pocket costs are lower and quality and experience don't suffer."[2] The PwC report was penned before the COVID-19 pandemic disrupted the global healthcare ecosystem. That disruption has put telemedicine and other forms of remote care in an entirely different light.

To answer the question, Is digital reconstruction necessary?, we address the following questions:

- Are digital health initiatives effective?
- Is episodic healthcare meeting patients' needs?
- How are healthcare needs being met in countries with a less-than-optimal healthcare infrastructure?
- Do we need a digitally enhanced clinical decision support system (CDSS) to address the epidemic of diagnostic errors?
- Will the COVID-19 pandemic require more online solutions?

Reviewing the Evidence on Effectiveness

The evidence to support the cost effectiveness of digital systems such as telemedicine, hospital at-home programs, remote patient monitoring, and mobile health apps is mixed. A 2013 analysis found the average cost of an in-person acute care visit for patients with private insurance was $136 to $176, whereas a similar telemedicine consultation was $40 to $50.[4] More recently, an analysis found that follow-up patient care after elective surgery may be more cost effective when telemedicine services are used. When 1,200 post-neurosurgical patients in India received either remote care or in-person care over 52 months, remote patient monitoring was deemed more effective and less expensive. The improvement was attributed in part to patients not having to travel to a medical facility for care.[5] Among patients with type 2 diabetes, mobile health interventions were likewise found cost effective in a 2020 systematic review of 23 studies. Rinaldi et al. cautioned, however: "Cost of mHealth interventions varied substantially based on type and combination of technology used . . ."[6]

One of the largest analyses of digital health companies, on the other hand, concluded that their services have yet to provide a "substantial impact on disease burden or cost in the US healthcare system" among patients with high-burden, expensive medical conditions.[7] Safavi et al. studied digital health vendors such as Jawbone, which provides biosensors to patients; Health Catalyst, a healthcare analytics firm that provides services to hospitals; Weltok, which offers population health management; Sharecare, which focuses on consumer health engagement; Accolade, a telemedicine service; and Doximity, a social networking service for physicians.

The observation that 104 analyzed studies did not demonstrate a meaningful impact on clinical outcomes or cost can be attributed to a "sin of omission." Only 27.9% of the studies looked at high-burden conditions, and none measured costs. Thus, it is impossible to conclude that the 20 top digital health companies studied have no effect on cost effectiveness, only that we do not yet know what impact they have because investigators have not been looking at the right metrics. In other words, a lack of evidence is not equivalent to negative evidence. The interventions provided by these and many other vendors and healthcare providers have the potential to improve clinical outcomes and costs because they improve care coordination, improve patient engagement, offer actionable insights for advanced data analytics, and much more.

A systematic review of 39 studies from 19 countries that examined mobile health interventions rather than digital health companies concluded that mHealth was cost effective, economically beneficial, or cost saving.[8] The analysis looked at a wide array of digital solutions, as illustrated in Figure 1.1. Among the 34 studies that evaluated these mHealth programs in upper- and upper-middle-income countries, 70.6% reported positive costing outcomes. In the 5 lower-middle and lower-income countries, all reported positive costing outcomes. The vast majority of the 39 analyses used behavior change communication approaches and found high rates of positive outcomes. These included programs that attempted to improve attendance and medication adherence. SMS was the most frequently used intervention, which was used to send appointment reminders, provide patient support, conduct surveys, and collect data. Among the studies that looked at SMS, 4 focused on diabetes management or prevention, and all 4 were deemed cost effective.

Several investigators have reviewed the evidence specifically supporting telemedicine services. The challenge in interpreting this evidence is the same as the challenge of interpreting studies in clinical medicine, namely, one size does not fit all. In controlled trials that examine the effectiveness of a treatment protocol for treating cardiovascular disease, for instance, a trial may conclude that a drug or lifestyle intervention is ineffective across the entire patient population, but that does not rule out its value in certain subgroups. Similarly, when reviewing telemedicine services, it is tempting to lump all services together or to treat different patient cohorts as one homogenous group. But it is far more likely that the benefits or harm caused by telemedicine varies depending on the type of disorder being treated, the severity of the disease, the communication tools being employed, the type of teleservice—asynchronous or synchronous—the state law governing the patient/clinician interaction, and whether service was offered directly to patients or to other clinicians as a tele-consultation. For example, tele-consultation has been shown to improve asthma control and quality of life when it was compared to routine care. But single case tele-care management failed to improve asthma control.[9] Similarly, telehealth care in which nurses contacted patients by phone was no more effective than in-person care. On the other hand, combining telecare with other approaches was found useful. For example, linking self-monitoring of asthma symptoms with the help of a

Type	Definition of application	Examples of activities
Behavior Change Communication (BCC) or Social BCC	Provide health information and behavior change messages directly to clients or the general public and help link people with services. Message content may increase individuals' knowledge or influence their attitudes and behaviors.	• Appointment reminders • Support for medication adherence • Promote healthy behavior (e.g. smoking cessation) • Community mobilization • Awareness-raising, education • Apps to support self-management
Information systems / Data collection	Increase the speed, reliability, quality, and accuracy of data collected through electronic methods and send to various levels of health system (district, state, national) for quicker analysis compared to paper-based systems.	• Collection and reporting of patient health and service provision • Electronic health records (EHR) • Registries, vital events tracking, surveillance and household surveys
Logistics / Supply management	Help track and manage commodities, prevent stock-outs, and facilitate equipment maintenance. Transmit information from lower-level to higher level health facility.	• Ensure medicines and basic supplies are in stock
Service delivery	Support health worker performance related to diagnosis, treatment, disease management and referrals, as well as preventive services. Provide decision support to patients.	• Electronic decision support, point of care tools, checklists, diagnostic tools, treatment algorithms • Improve communication: provider-provider, provider-patient (notify test results, follow-up visits)
Financial transactions and incentives	Improve access to health services, expedite payments to providers and health services, and reduce cash-based operating costs.	• Load/transfer/withdraw money, savings accounts, and insurance • Performance-based incentives, vouchers for services (e.g., family planning and antenatal services)
Workforce development and support	Facilitate training and education, provider work planning and scheduling, supportive supervision, and human resource management.	• Train and retain health care workers, provide education

Note. Adapted from the Global Health Learning Center mHealth Basics, USAID (2014) and mHealth Compendium (2015)

doi:10.1371/journal.pone.0170581.t001

Figure 1.1 Mobile Health Interventions. The digital health options available to clinicians and patients include basic tools, such as appointment reminders and more advanced systems that provide clinical decision support. (*Source:* Iribarren SJ, Cato K, Falzon L, Stone PW. What is the economic evidence for mHealth? A systematic review of economic evaluations of mHealth solutions. *PLOS ONE.* 2017;12:e0170581. doi:10.1371/journal.pone.0170581[8])

Web-based questionnaire with feedback from clinicians, in conjunction with a weekly lung function assessment that prompted a clinical visit when needed, did improve asthma control. Likewise, giving patients an application that monitored their symptoms and combining it with 2-way text messaging and a medication diary generated positive outcomes. For a more in-depth review of the evidence on telemedicine, see Chapter 5.

There is also evidence to suggest that hospital at-home programs are clinically and cost effective. Bruce Leff, MD, at Johns Hopkins Hospital, has done much of the groundbreaking research in this area. He and his colleagues evaluated such a program in 455 elderly patients in 3 Medicare-managed systems and a VA medical center and found positive results. "On an intention-to-treat basis, patients treated in hospital-at-home had a shorter length of stay (3.2 vs. 4.9 days) (P = 0.004), and there was some evidence that they also had fewer complications. The mean cost was lower for hospital-at-home care than for acute hospital care ($5,081 vs. $7,480) ($P$ < 0.001)."[10] Mayo Clinic and several other large healthcare systems are currently investigating similar models, which we will discuss at greater length in Chapter 5.

Episodic Medical Care Often Falls Short

White coat hypertension, the tendency for patients to only present with elevated blood pressure during a doctor visit, illustrates a problem that permeates the entire healthcare ecosystem. Any sign or symptom that a patient exhibits during an office or clinic visit may not be a true presentation of their underlying condition. Unfortunately, this phenomenon not only affects a person's blood pressure but other common parameters. White coat hyperglycemia has also been documented.[11] And since psychosocial stress is likely a contributing cause of such white coat reactions, white coat hypercholesterolemia, asthma attacks, and numerous other conditions probably exist as well, all triggered by stress hormones. Conversely, any normal readings during a physical examination or laboratory test do not necessarily mean a patient is in good health.

The common denominator in all these scenarios is episodic care. In such situations, clinicians are making a judgement about a patient's health status based on cross-sectional data, which can be misleading. But given the financial restraints and incentives that exist in healthcare today, it has been the only viable option—until now. With the emergence of virtual care and remote patient monitoring (RPM), gathering long-term data for many clinical parameters is no longer out of reach. That steady stream of online data can be inserted into predictive analytics algorithms to help locate patients at high risk. Some thought leaders refer to this shift in priorities as the movement from episodic to *life-based care.* Judy Murphy, RN, the chief nursing officer at IBM Global Healthcare, points out that using the data generated from RPM allows clinicians to find those patients most likely to require catastrophic care. She has found that a substantial number of patients are very willing to engage with the healthcare system using patient portals and other resources, but for others, "it's up to healthcare to review the available data and engage at-risk individuals before they join the small portion of critical patients that are driving costs."[12]

Such digitally enhanced patient engagement is the future of healthcare. No responsible practitioner would conclude a diabetic patient is in good metabolic control based on a single blood glucose reading, and yet that is often the same reasoning we use when a routine metabolic panel comes back stating LDL cholesterol, serum calcium, white blood count, blood pressure, and numerous other parameters are all "within reference range." We now have the technology to move beyond this outdated mindset. That technology enables us to detect longitudinal patterns of change in patients' health status. By way of example: Longitudinal data on systolic blood pressure has been linked to patients' risk of cardiovascular disease.[13]

Diagnostic Errors, Inadequate Infrastructure

The epidemic of diagnostic errors that exists in medicine also demands that we embrace digital reconstruction. In our last book, *Reinventing Clinical Decision Support,*[14] we cited the statistics on the problem. A 2015 report from the National Academy of Medicine points out that about 5% of adult outpatients in the United States experience a diagnostic error annually.[15] The same report found that diagnostic mishaps contribute to about 1 out of 10 patient deaths, cause as much as 17% of hospital adverse effects, and affect approximately 12 million adult outpatients a year, which translates into 1 out of 20 Americans. About half of these errors may be harmful, according to Singh.[16] Among the 850,000 patients who have died in US hospitals annually, about 71,400 of these deaths included a major diagnosis that had not been detected.

The list of contributing causes for such diagnostic errors is long and includes:

- Failure of patients to engage with a provider organization or to participate in the diagnostic process (ignoring patient input regarding signs and symptoms)
- Inadequate collection of relevant patient information
- Inadequate knowledge base among clinicians

- Incorrect interpretation of medical information (e.g., cognitive errors and biases)
- Failure to integrate collected medical information into a plausible diagnostic hypothesis (e.g., cognitive errors and biases)

Many of these issues can be addressed with CDSSs and machine learning (ML), as we will discuss in subsequent chapters.

The poorly constructed healthcare infrastructure that exists in many countries is one more reason to consider digital solutions. In China, for example, few patients have access to primary care physicians, and, as a result, specialists and hospital clinics are overwhelmed with patients who do not really need the specialized care. Part of the country's effort to reinvent its healthcare ecosystem includes the introduction of a digital health initiative called Ping An Good Doctor, which has enrolled over 300 million citizens. Ping An offers telemedicine services, working with local governments and rural clinics to meet the population's needs.

Digital Health During Times of Crisis

As we go to press, the COVID-19 pandemic is arguably the most compelling reason to explore the digital reconstruction of healthcare. This international crisis has forced executives, vendors, clinicians, and patients to reevaluate the need for face-to-face consultations, which has made telemedicine, home care services, and remote patient monitoring not only appealing but life-saving in many situations. So, although the published data on the clinical and cost effectiveness of these services remains inconclusive to date, the global threat of the pandemic has resulted in a worldwide natural experiment that will ultimately determine the merits of digital health.

Digital tools can serve several functions during the pandemic. For anyone monitoring their own health and wondering whether they are experiencing the early signs and symptoms of the infection, remote sensing devices, including a digital thermometer and pulse oximeter, provide objective data to help them determine if they need to contact a health professional or seek emergency care. A low-grade fever or oxygen saturation readings below 93% may be cause for concern. At the very least, this information can be used during a phone conversation with one's primary care provider to help them evaluate the need for further action. Secondly, RPM devices can be used during a telemedicine visit to guide clinician's diagnostic reasoning. Adult patients with COVID-19 who have pneumonia may present with SpO2 at or below 93%, even in the absence of shortness of breath.[17] Finally, online services can assist in contact tracing during the pandemic. Once a patient has been identified as being COVID positive, health officials and volunteers in many communities are asking the patient to provide a list of persons who they have been in close contact with. Those individuals are then contacted and instructed to self-isolate until it is safe for them to go out in public again. The state of Massachusetts is piloting an automated exposure notification system to enhance its manual community-tracing collaborative. It will enlist the help of numerous stakeholders, including the Commonwealth of Massachusetts Department of Public Health, the MITRE Corporation, Mayo Clinic, MIT, Google, and Apple. Chapter 3 will explore the value of such digital services in detecting and managing COVID-19 in more detail.

Digital health solutions may not offer the panacea suggested by some overly enthusiastic advocates and entrepreneurs, but the evidence indicates they need to become an essential part of the healthcare ecosystem. The suggestive evidence supporting its clinical and cost effectiveness, coupled with the inadequacies of episodic care, the 12 to 18 million diagnostic errors each year, and the life-threatening risks associated with COVID-19 require that we give up the status quo mentality that has stifled innovation for so many decades.

References

1. Belmonte A. America's 'inefficient' health care system is driving fiscal instability: Powell. *Yahoo Finance*. Feb 26, 2019. https://finance.yahoo.com/news/america-health-care-system-unsustainable-171558952.html
2. PwC Health Research Institute. Medical cost trend: behind the numbers 2020. June 2019. https://www.pwc.com/us/en/industries/health-industries/assets/pwc-hri-behind-the-numbers-2020.pdf
3. Schneider EC, Squires D. From last to first—could the U.S. healthcare system become the best in the world? *The Commonwealth Fund*. July 17, 2017. https://www.commonwealthfund.org/publications/journal-article/2017/jul/last-first-could-us-health-care-system-become-best-world?redirect_source=/publications/in-brief/2017/jul/last-to-first-could-us-health-system-become-best-in-world
4. Yamamoto DH. Assessment of the feasibility and cost of replacing in-person care with acute care telehealth services. Red Quill Consulting. 2014. http://connectwithcare.org/wp-content/uploads/2014/12/Medicare-Acute-Care-Telehealth-Feasibility.pdf
5. Thakar S, Rajagopal N, Mani S, et al. Comparison of telemedicine with in-person care for follow-up after elective neurosurgery: results of a cost-effectiveness analysis of 1200 patients using patient-perceived utility scores. *Neurosurg Focus*. 2018;44:E17.

6. Rinaldi G, Hijazi A, Haghparast-Bidgoli H. Cost and cost-effectiveness of mHealth interventions for the prevention and control of type 2 diabetes mellitus: a systematic review. *Diabetes Res Clin Pract.* 2020;162:108084.

7. Safavi K. Mathews SC, Bates DW, et al. Top-funded digital health companies and their impact on high-burden, high-cost conditions. *Health Affairs.* 2019; 38:115–123.

8. Iribarren SJ, Cato K, Falzon L, Stone PW. What is the economic evidence for mHealth? A systematic review of economic evaluations of mHealth solutions. *PLOS ONE.* 2017;12: e0170581. doi:10.1371/journal.pone.0170581

9. Portnoy JM, Wu AC. Is telemedicine as effective as usual care? *J Allergy Clin Immunol Pract.* 2019;7:217–218.

10. Leff B, Burton L, Mader SL, et al. Hospital at home: feasibility and outcomes of a program to provide hospital-level care at home for acutely ill older patients. *Ann Intern Med.* 2005;143:798–808.

11. Benmoussa J, Clarke M, Bloomfield D. White coat hyperglycemia: the forgotten syndrome. *J Clin Med Res.* 2016 Aug;8(8):567–568.

12. Muoio D. Healthcare is moving from episodic to "life-based care." *Healthcare IT News.* March 5, 2018. https://www.healthcareitnews.com/news/healthcare-moving -episodic-life-based-care

13. Petruski-Ivleva N, Viera AJ, Shimbo D, et al. Longitudinal patterns of change in systolic blood pressure and incidence of cardiovascular disease the atherosclerosis risk in communities study. *Hypertension.* 2016;67:1150–1156.

14. Cerrato P, Halamka J. *Reinventing Clinical Decision Support: Data Analytics, Artificial Intelligence, and Diagnostic Reasoning.* Boca Raton, FL: CRC Press/ Taylor and Francis Group; 2020.

15. National Academies of Sciences, Engineering, and Medicine. *Improving Diagnosis in Health Care.* Washington, DC: National Academies Press; 2015.

16. Singh, H. Editorial: Helping health care organizations to define diagnostic errors as missed opportunities in diagnosis." *Jt Comm J Qual Patient Saf.* 2014;40(3):99–101.

17. World Health Organization. Clinical management of severe acute respiratory infection (SARI) when COVID-19 disease is suspected: interim guidance. March 5, 2020. https://www.who.int/docs/default-source/coronaviruse/clinical -management-of-novel-cov.pdf. Accessed May 6, 2020.

Chapter 2

The Merits and Limitations of Telemedicine, Hospital at Home, and Remote Patient Monitoring

During a recent conversation with Rasu Shrestha, MD, chief strategy officer at Atrium Health in Charlotte, NC, he spoke of the building blocks that make up the current healthcare system, including electronic health record (EHR) systems, picture archive and communication systems (PACS), enterprise data warehouses, population health initiatives, and case management. EHR systems, for example, were originally designed to manage medical billing and documentation. This functionality is certainly inadequate in today's healthcare system. "Today we really want a platform that allows for ongoing conversations around the patient's journey," says Dr. Shrestha. EHRs are not especially conversational. Many forward-thinking providers have begun using a variety of telemedicine services, two-way texting tools, digital add-ons and apps, and non-digital tools such as telephone follow-ups to improve the doctor/patient relationship. Unfortunately, these tools are not a routine part of the healthcare ecosystem, either in the United States or in many other countries. Nor are they built into many commercially available EHRs.

With these challenges in mind, our goal here is to envision an ecosystem that takes full advantage of the latest technologies, including the best that telemedicine, hospital at home, and remote patient monitoring can offer.

Telemedicine's Dramatic Growth

The COVID-19 pandemic has reshaped patient care in ways that were unimaginable until very recently. For example, telemedicine urgent care visits at NYU Langone Health increased from 102.4 daily visits on March 2, 2020 to 801.6 visits on April 14th.[1] This 683% increase mirrors the dramatic increases seen by many other healthcare systems. It is not possible to know with certainty how long this spike in telemedicine usage will last. It is likely it will diminish once the pandemic has subsided but unlikely to return to the same low level that existed before the health crisis began. In fact, the pandemic probably represents a turning point in telemedicine in terms of clinicians' and patients' willingness to engage with the technology.

Consider the statistics: In the past, most states required a physician providing telemedicine services be licensed in the same state as the patient he or she is treating, have a preexisting relationship with the patient, and/or only be allowed to conduct an audio consultation. As of May 26, 2020, 49 states, Guam, and Puerto Rico have waived some or all of these requirements during the COVID-19 pandemic.[2] Many states are also making it easier for providers and patients seeking third-party reimbursement. The American Medical Association's Advocacy Resource Center outlines the state directives that have expanded telemedicine services during the pandemic, including directives to provide insurance coverage parity and payment parity.[3] In Maryland, for example, "Insurers must reimburse for the diagnosis, consultation and treatment that can be appropriately provided through telehealth." In Michigan, the state mandates "Coverage and payment the same as if the service were provided in person; audio only allowed."

The federal government has also made allowances for telemedicine services during the pandemic. The U.S. Department of Health and Human Services has loosened restrictions to allow more opportunities for clinicians to receive reimbursement through the Medicare and Medicaid programs. Before the government waiver, only physicians, nurse practitioners, physician assistants, and certain other providers were permitted to deliver Medicare telehealth services. During the COVID pandemic, the interim policy now includes "all practitioners eligible to bill Medicare for professional services, including physical therapists, occupational therapists, and speech language pathologists, etc." The agency has also allowed remote physiological monitoring services for the purposes of treating suspected COVID-19 infections, stating that such services can be reported to Medicare for periods of time that are fewer than 16 to 30 days but no less than 2 days, assuming other billing code requirements have been met.[4,5]

Several healthcare analysts and consulting firms have weighed in on the post COVID-19 telemedicine scenario. McKinsey & Company estimates that spending on telemedicine may reach up to $250 billion in the United States.[6] Bestsennyy et al. envision 5 possible models for telemedicine, as well as several potential barriers to implementation:

- On-demand virtual urgent care
- Virtual office visits
- Near-virtual office visits
- Virtual home health services
- Technology-enabled home medication administration

Among the barriers and challenges that can short-circuit any of these approaches are poor security, inadequate integration into clinicians' workflow, lack of equitable reimbursement, liability and malpractice lawsuits, and questionable effectiveness. Ignoring the public's growing enthusiasm for telemedicine, on the other hand, may put provider organizations at a competitive disadvantage if they have to contend with nearby clinics that offer one-off, quick online services.

On-demand virtual care visits could replace about one in five emergency department (ED) visits, according to a McKinsey claims analysis, and would be a viable substitute for low-acuity ED visits, in-person visits to an urgent care center, and after-hours consultations. One disadvantage to this model is that it would connect patients with an unfamiliar provider. Virtual office visits, on the other hand, would link patients to their established clinician and could replace many in-person primary care visits for chronic conditions, in-person psychotherapy, and certain types of specialty care. This approach would also be a good fit for remote patient monitoring using a variety of digital tools currently on the market, including otoscopes, pulse oximeters, blood pressure cuffs, digital thermometers, one-lead EKG devices, and body-weight scales.

The near-virtual office visit model envisions a combination of online visits with in-person trips to nearby testing sites where patients can have blood drawn, receive vaccinations, and other services that cannot be performed over the Internet. Virtual home health services would provide a vehicle for patients to receive education and professionally guided physical and occupational therapy; home medication administration would allow select patients to receive infusible and injectable drugs at home rather than in a clinic. It could also allow oncologists to virtually monitor a nurse administrating chemotherapy in the patient's home.

The McKinsey analysis offers several practical suggestions to turn these models into everyday clinical realities. Insurers are encouraged to rethink how they reimburse for patient care by accelerating "value-based contracting to incentivize telehealth" and by developing new insurance products that meet the growing public demand for such online services. Similarly, third-party payors need to build the technology and analytics supporting their telemedicine offerings. Among the recommendations offered to healthcare providers: Segment patient populations to determine which portions of your patients with chronic diseases would benefit most from telemedicine visits. Although the McKinsey report does not specifically mention women's health, obstetric/gynecologic patients are a good fit for telemed services. In fact, the American College of Obstetricians and Gynecologists recently published a committee opinion that states: "Telehealth is increasingly used in every aspect of obstetrics and gynecology. Obstetrician-gynecologists and other physicians should consider becoming familiar with and adept in this new technology."[7] The McKinsey analysis also recommends that providers encourage their workforce to buy into the telemedicine model by implementing better workflow design, centralized scheduling, and continuing education.

The Advisory Board, another prominent consulting firm, offered additional insights in its post COVID-19 assessment of telemedicine.[8] Like many other analysts, the Board has called attention to the uncertain reimbursement policies once the pandemic lifts. As of June 2020, the Centers for Medicare and Medicaid Services (CMS) had agreed to suspend more than 89 regulations that had been blocking reimbursement at the same rate as the agency allowed for in-person visits. If CMS rescinds these changes, "the industry will find itself right back where it was before COVID-19." But given the new enthusiasm among the public since they experienced telemedicine services, it seems unlikely the federal government will revoke all the new allowances. One survey found that 69% of consumers want their healthcare providers to offer more telemedicine services as an alternative to in-person visits once the pandemic is over. In addition, about one third of consumers don't feel safe going to a hospital since the pandemic began. It's likely that fear will have a long shelf life.[8]

What is not likely to disappear is clinicians' impatience with the less-than-optimal technology required to use telemedicine services. Many providers have yet to integrate their telemed services into their EHR systems, requiring practitioners to switch back and forth between applications. If we are going to make telemedicine an easy-to-use service line, this stumbling block needs to be addressed. And once EHR and telemed services are integrated, it should also be possible to connect the combined service to remote monitoring devices, lab results, imaging services, and referrals.

The shift to such online services will also require decision makers to rethink any plans to embark on new construction projects. After all, if more patients will be seen in virtual clinics, many brick-and-mortar facilities will go the way of the Blockbuster video stores and many book and record shops.

Making Informed Telemed Choices

Many healthcare providers were interested in expanding their telemedicine services even before the COVID-19 pandemic emerged. In the post-COVID world, that interest will only grow. Healthcare systems that do not want to create their own telemed service from the ground up will need to evaluate the commercially available platforms to find the right fit. That fit will depend on both clinician and patient needs and preferences.

In the brick-and-mortar world, physicians are accustomed to having support staff handle many of the administrative duties associated with patient care, including patient scheduling, collecting of insurance information, gathering basic demographic details, collecting symptom lists, and the like. How many of these responsibilities will the clinician be required to navigate and how much is built into the infrastructure of the vendor's product? Similarly, is there a structure in place to help triage patients? With advances in chatbot technology, it is now possible for many patients to be screened for minor problems through an automated conversation that routes more urgent issues to practitioners with the right qualifications.

On the patient side of the equation, provider organizations need to consider the complexity of getting technology-naïve patients through the initial setup. Is the registration process simple enough? Does the patient have to download an app and then configure it in ways that will confuse them? Are there "safety valves" in place to ensure that patients with serious signs and symptoms are shunted to appropriate care?

Forrester Research has outlined several additional selection criteria to assist providers as they evaluate telemedicine services, including[9]:

- Network support
- Interoperability
- Performance metrics
- Market approach
- The vendor's vision

Using a long list of criteria, Forrester ranked several telemedicine vendors. The firm evaluated 13 companies—98point6, American Well, Bright.md, CirrusMD, Doctor On Demand, eVisit Telemedicine Solution, InTouch Technologies, MDLIVE, SnapMD, Synzi, Teladoc Health, TytoCare, and Zipnosis—giving its highest grade to Bright.md and listing Teladoc Health, InTouch Technologies, and 98point 6 as strong performers. Zipnosis, MDLive, Doctor on Demand, American Well, and eVisit Telemedicine were ranked as "Contenders."

Of course, this kind of analysis cannot compare to a detailed, individualized review, which can only be performed by a healthcare provider's own team. That customized review has to include a review of the relevant state laws on telemedicine and consultation with one's malpractice insurer as well as the billing department. On a related note, in January 2019, CMS released new billing codes that support reimbursement for remote patient monitoring: 99453, 99454, 99457, and 99458. Joseph Kvedar, MD, the president of the American Telemedicine Association, has complied a detailed explanation of how to interpret and utilize these codes. Details on those codes are discussed below in the section on remote patient monitoring (RPM).

To navigate the telemedicine vendor landscape, the American Medical Association (AMA) provides an in-depth guide: *Telehealth Implementation Playbook*.[10] This comprehensive document, written in the midst of the COVID-19 pandemic, walks users through the entire acquisition and implementation process, including continuity of care, licensure, and reimbursement; a "pre-game" evaluation of an organization's needs; overcoming barriers; contracting and vendor evaluation; "game time," which dives into designing workflow; preparing the care team and patient; implementation; scaling; and how to judge whether the program is successful. A list of resources include the CMS billing codes mentioned above, best practices, and use cases.

Examining the Scientific Evidence

Numerous studies have addressed the clinical and cost effectiveness of telemedicine. Sarah Wild, with the Usher Institute of Population Health Sciences and Informatics, University of Edinburgh, and colleagues have tested the value of telemonitoring in patients with poorly controlled type 2 diabetes. Using Bluetooth technology paired with portable glucose meters, patients sent their readings to a remote server monitored by nurses. When HbA1c data was tabulated from 146 patients in the experimental program and from 139 controls, the researchers discovered that the readings declined by a clinically significant 0.51% in the telemonitored patients (63 vs. 67.8 mmol/mol or 8.9% vs. 9.4%).[11]

When evaluating such studies, it is important to consider methodology and context. Wild et al. used well-trained research nurses working with established family practices; they were required to adhere to ethical standards and conducted a well-controlled multicenter randomized trial. Resneck et al., on the other hand, studied direct-to-consumer (DTC) telemedicine websites and smartphone apps claiming the ability to diagnose and treat skin disease, with disappointing results.[12] Jack Resneck and associates used simulated case reports of imaginary patients with various disorders and sent them to several DTC services in California, including DermatologistOnCall, Dermcheck, DermLink, Direct Dermatology, First Derm, SkyMD, Spruce, Virtual Acne, YoDerm, Amwell, First Opinion, HealthTap Prime, MDLive, MeMD, Teladoc, and Virtuwell. Seventeen services responded; many of the responses fell short of accepted medical standards for dermatological care. For example, only 26% of the telemedicine services informed simulated patients that they used licensed clinicians, and some used clinicians outside the United States who did not have a license to practice in the state of California. Only 10% offered to send the patient's records to their primary care physician. "Major diagnoses were repeatedly missed, including secondary syphilis, eczema herpeticum, gram-negative folliculitis, and polycystic ovarian syndrome." Equally important was the discovery that some of the prescribed treatments did not conform to clinical guidelines.

Schoenfeld et al. reported similar variations in quality of care delivered by on-demand telemedicine from commercial services.[13] They submitted fictitious patient scenarios to 8 popular on-demand services, seeking care for 6 common conditions: ankle pain, streptococcal pharyngitis, viral pharyngitis, acute rhinosinusitis, low back pain, and recurrent urinary tract infection; about 600 virtual visits were generated. They found that about 1 in 4 "patients" received an incorrect diagnosis, and clinical guidelines were adhered to only 54.3% of the time. Such adherence varied widely for viral pharyngitis and acute rhinosinusitis (12.8% to 82.1%). Variations for ankle pain and recurrent urinary tract infection were 3.4% to 40.4%. Although these findings are troublesome, one must compare such variations to those found in brick-and-mortar clinical settings, in which researchers have likewise reported considerable variations in quality of care and adherence to guidelines.

These findings are in stark contrast to those reported by pediatric researchers using a telemedicine service provided by an Israeli healthcare system.[14] Two physicians reviewed 339 randomly selected cases and found diagnoses were appropriate in 98.5%. False positives were only 2.65%, and false negatives, 5.3%. The analysis also compared clinicians' decisions to follow up outcomes and found a strong correlation between online decisions and outcomes, including parental adherence to recommendations and medical follow-ups within the healthcare system. A closer look at the type of service provided explain the different results: Physicians who were providing the telemedicine services, which was delivered by telephone or live video chat, had access to the childrens' medical records, including lab data and imaging. They could also tap into information about patients' previous visits to community clinics, emergency departments, and hospitals. In addition, all the providers were experienced pediatricians or subspecialists, and they had previous experience using telemedicine. Using all these advantages, the clinicians were able to direct patients most in need of immediate care to receive quick treatment and allow those who did not require an ED visit to avoid it.

Positive results were also reported by the University of New Mexico, which used video conferencing to treat patients in underserved communities who had a hepatitis C virus (HCV) infection.[15] Arora et al. employed the Extension for Community Healthcare Outcomes (ECHO) model, which has been specifically designed to improve rural minority patients' access to best practice care for HCV. To test the effectiveness of the model, they compared traditional care at primary care clinics to 21 ECHO sites in rural areas and prisons in New Mexico. About 57% of clinic patients and 58% of ECHO patients experienced a sustained viral response (P = 0.89), whereas serious adverse events occurred in 13.7% of clinic patients compared to only 6.9% in patients receiving virtual care. Once again, it is important to emphasize the detailed training and expertise that goes into such successful online initiatives. Arora et al. explain:

> *Community providers take part in weekly HCV clinics, called "knowledge networks," by joining a video conference or calling into a teleconference line . . . The providers present their cases by sharing patients' medical histories, laboratory results, treatment plans, and individual challenges and ask questions about best practices. Specialists at the UNM Health Sciences Center from the fields of hepatology, infectious diseases, psychiatry, and pharmacology provide advice and clinical mentoring during these clinics. Working together, the community providers and specialists manage the patients' care according to evidence-based protocols. These case-based discussions are supplemented with short didactic presentations by interdisciplinary experts to improve content knowledge.*

Many DTC telemedicine services, on the other hand, do not offer the same level of care. Consumers can now find ads for DTC services that boast "the erectile dysfunction meds you definitely don't need, but your 'friend' was asking about," and online services that offer an easy way to obtain a prescription for oral contraceptives and other medications.[16] All too often, these services do not even require a direct conversation between clinician and patient but rather just a questionnaire for patients to fill out. That begs the question: Are these patients receiving the kind of care that includes a review of possible contraindications for said medications. Jain et al. point out: "[T]he American Urological Association guidelines state that men with erectile dysfunction require a targeted physical examination. In addition, DTC telemedicine companies may lead to further fragmentation of health care and not all companies offer the option to forward the visit summary to the patient's primary care physician."

Investigations that have evaluated cost effectiveness have also been revealing. Oksmen et al.[17] conducted blinded, randomized trials of 1570 primary care patients with chronic conditions. During a 12-month period, the intervention group received telephone coaching from nurses specifically trained to perform motivational interviewing, whereas controls received routine care. Cost effectiveness was most pronounced among patients with type 2 diabetes but more modest in those with coronary artery disease. Patients with congestive heart failure actually experienced an increase in costs and no improvement in quality of care.

Telemedicine's Limitations and Obstacles

Despite many encouraging reports of the benefits of telemedicine, it would be naïve to conclude that all segments of the population benefit equally from such services. These disparities have only become more acute during the COVID-19 pandemic. In the United States, Congress passed the Coronavirus Aid, Relief, and Economic Security (CARES) Act, which allocates over $1 billion to address such disparities, but such efforts have fallen short in rural and other underserved areas.

Community health centers (CHCs) were designed to address the needs of these groups. A 2018 analysis from the Uniform Data System found almost half (565) of 1,330 CHCs had no telehealth services. And among those centers that did have telehealth, nearly half (47%) only used it to communicate with specialists, not patients.[18] Among the significant barriers to telemedicine implementation in CHCs: lack of reimbursement and funding for equipment, and inadequate staff training.

Another concern among healthcare providers is the possible overutilization of medical services that may result from wide use of telemedicine. Investigators from the University of Wisconsin and University of Pennsylvania found that e-visits actually increase the number of office visits, by 6%.[19] That conclusion was based on an analysis of a dataset of several hospitals, medical centers, and medical practices and over 2.5 million primary care visits. Similarly, a RAND Corporation study reviewed insurance claims data from more than 300,000 patients over a 3-year period and found that about 12% of DTC telehealth visits had replaced regular medical visits, but 88% represented new utilization. The results suggest that "increased convenience may tap into unmet demand for health care, and new utilization may increase overall health care spending."[20]

One final word of caution on telemedicine: The expanded use of telemedicine services that has occurred during the COVID-19 pandemic has resulted in part from the loosening of regulations and protocols. These changes are a double-edged sword. Keeping in mind Newton's third law of motion—for every action there is an equal but opposite reaction—the healthcare industry will likely see pushback from all these accommodations. Although these accommodations have allowed many patients to gain much-needed medical care, once the pandemic recedes and the urgency of seeing as many patients as quickly as possible wanes, these loosened restrictions on patient privacy, online security, state licensure laws, and the like will probably expose sensitive health information from some patients and allow some healthcare providers' networks to be hacked. When that happens, any resulting lawsuits or harm to patients, and clinicians may have headline-grabbing consequences. Should that occur, it could force regulators, insurers, patients and clinicians to return to the same overly cautious postures that prevailed before COVID-19. To avoid that eventuality, Healthcare Information and Management Systems Society (HIMSS) standards and related safeguards need to be restored and reimagined as soon as possible.

These concerns are not mere academic speculation, as evidenced by a Black Hat survey conducted during the pandemic. Black Hat Briefings have been providing cybersecurity specialists with the latest vendor neutral threat assessment data for over 20 years. A survey of Black Hat USA conference current and former attendees[21] found that 94% believe the pandemic increases the cyberthreat to enterprise systems and data. "The experts point to changes stemming from the need to social distance as a source of potential threats, with 72% saying they were concerned about quarantined home workers breaking policy and exposing systems to risk."[22] As in the past, one of the chief concerns is phishing emails, in which gullible employees click on seemingly harmless links and attachments that send them to websites that, in turn, download malware to their computer network. The economic upheaval that has accompanied COVID-19 will likewise contribute to data breaches because few healthcare organizations can afford to bolster their network with much-needed technology.

Remote Patient Monitoring

Many patients and healthcare professionals have yet to appreciate the power of remote patient monitoring. When executed correctly, it can be truly transformative, combining medical self-care, objective physiological data, and expert advice to improve both preventive and therapeutic care. And as RPM continues to mature, it has the potential to completely reinvent healthcare, especially among those motivated patients who see it as a source of self-empowerment.

The power of RPM in the hands of motivated asthmatic patients was well illustrated in an experiment conducted by University of Wisconsin and Centers for Disease Control and Prevention researchers.[23] Using an electronic medication sensor (Figure 2.1) that was attached to inhalers of 30 patients, Van Sickle et al. tracked patients' use of inhaled short-acting bronchodilators for 4 months.

Figure 2.1 GPS-enabled inhaler sensor attached to inhaled albuterol used by patients who received email reports and online charts documenting their use of bronchodilator medication. (*Source:* Van Sickle D, Magzamen S, Truelove S, Morrison T. Remote monitoring of inhaled bronchodilator use and weekly feedback about asthma management: an open-group, short-term pilot study of the impact on asthma control. *PLOS ONE.* 2013;8:e55335.[23])

To evaluate patients' health status, investigators asked them to fill out surveys, including the Asthma Control Test (ACT). One month into the study, they also received weekly emails that summed up their medication usage for the preceding week and offered suggestions on how to comply with the National Asthma Education and Prevention Program guidelines. No changes were observed in ACT scores after the first month, but they increased by 1.40 points each month after that. Patients also reported significant decreases in daytime and nighttime symptoms. They also noted "increased awareness and understanding of asthma patterns, level of control, bronchodilator use (timing, location) and triggers, and improved preventive practices." That last statement is worth closer inspection. Very often, patients do not understand the triggers that cause symptoms, unless they are actually attuned to subtle changes in their physiology. Providing graphic displays of their symptoms paired with the medication usage can be eye-opening for many patients who never noticed patterns of use before. These new-found revelations were summed up by several patients participating in the study:

"I learned that I used my inhaler more than I remember. I was able to see and relate to my doctor that my asthma is not under control." Participants also reported that the receipt of information about the time and location where they used their inhaler helped to highlight locations and exposures to triggers that led to symptoms. "I've been more keen to note surroundings when I feel shortness of breath," one participant said. "It opened my eyes to triggers I wasn't aware of in the past."

The results of this experiment highlight 2 important lessons for patients and clinicians, summed up in a few choice words from Kamal Jethwani, MD, MPH, from Partners HealthCare: "The future of health is proactive, self-managed wellness. We want to put the onus back on the person. We're saying: It's your health, and I'm no longer your babysitter."[24]

Since that 2013 experiment was published, numerous vendors have entered the RPM market to address the needs of patients with respiratory disorders. Kathleen Fan and her colleagues at the University of California San Diego have reviewed the latest digital tools designed to help monitor and predict COPD flare-ups. Their findings, summarized in Figure 2.2, included an evaluation of their forecasting ability, cost, ease of use, and appearance. Forecasting ability was defined as "the likelihood the device would signal a developing COPD exacerbation based on indicative biomarkers." Spirometers, pulse oximeters, and the Propeller Health sensor received the poorest predictive scores, whereas more sophisticated, albeit more expensive, devices such as Spry Health Loop System, Spire Health Tag, Adamm RSM, and Current Health Armband were given the top forecasting scores.[25] The Spry system consists of a wristband that tracks oxygen saturation, heart rate (HR), respiratory rate (RR), and blood pressure (BP), sending alerts to users when it detects significant changes in physiological parameters. Spire employs a disposable adhesive sensor that monitors HR, RR, breathing pattern, sleep quality, and physical activity, sending data to patients' smartphone app. The Adamm system is a device attached to the patient's upper torso to monitor cough rate, respiratory pattern, HR, and temperature. Current Health's system is an armband that measures HR, RR, skin temperature, oxygen saturation, and movement. The metrics are sent to a cloud platform and can be folded into a patient's EHR.

Such revelations are only the tip of the proverbial iceberg. A case report from HomeHealth Visiting Nurse, MaineHealth, documented improvements in hospital readmission rate, clinical outcomes, and patient satisfaction using a collection of RPM devices, including a wireless watch pedometer, glucose monitor, weight scale, and pulse oximeter among 275 patients with congestive heart failure, chronic obstructive pulmonary disease, and diabetes.[26] Over a 6-month period, the nursing team documented a drop in readmission rates from 11.3%

Figure 2.2 Comparison of selected chronic obstructive pulmonary disease handheld and hands-free remote monitors. (*Source:* Fan KG, Mandel J, Agnihotri P, et al. Remote patient monitoring technologies for predicting chronic obstructive pulmonary disease exacerbations: review and comparison. *JMIR MHealth and UHealth.* 2020;8:e16147.[25])

Device	Forecasting ability	Cost	Ease of use	Appearance
Handheld				
Spirometer	★	$99–$2500	★	★★★
Pulse oximeter	★	$15–$599	★	★
Propeller Health sensor	★	unlisted	★★★	★★★★
Cohero Health kit	★★★	$49/mo	★★★	★★★
Hands-free				
Spry Health Loop System	★★★★★	unlisted	★★★★★	★★★★★
Omron HeartGuide	★★★	$499	★★★★★	★★★★★
Spire Health Tag	★★★★★	$49	★★★	★★★★
Cosinuss One	★	$146.50	★★★	★★★
Current Health Armband	★★★★★	$199 + $40/mo	★★★	★
Adamm RSM	★★★★	unlisted	★★★★★	★★★★★

at 30 days postdischarge to 4.72% at 60 days and a patient adherence of 74.5% to 77%.

RPM not only has value among outpatients. Evidence suggests it can be effective within a hospital setting. Johns Hopkins Hospital[27] has used an infrared real-time location system (IR-RTLS) to track how much walking postoperative cardiac patients do before discharge and found that the detailed data generated on 100 patients predicted clinical outcomes, including 30-day readmission rate. The tracking system, which included a badge worn by each patient and sensors already embedded in hospital corridors, yielded a sensitivity of 86.7%, specificity 88.2%, and C-statistic of 0.925 for 30-day readmission. Similarly, results were observed for discharge to acute rehabilitation and length of stay.

The evidence documenting the value of RPM has prompted the CMS to release 3 billing codes in 2019. Code 99453 allows a payment of $19.46 for remote monitoring of biological markers, including weight, blood pressure, and pulse oximetry. It lets clinicians bill for initial setup and patient education on the use of the equipment. Code 99453 provides reimbursement when clinicians provide patients with an RPM device for 30 days. It allows billing for each 30-day period; average payment: $64.15. Code 99457 allows providers to bill for clinical staff time involved in managing RPM, including the use of phone, text, and email. Average payment is about $32–$51. Code 99091 pays for: "Collection and interpretation of physiologic data (e.g. ECG, blood pressure, glucose monitoring) digitally stored and/or transmitted by the patient and/or caregiver to the physician or other qualified healthcare professional, qualified by education, training, licensure/regulation (when applicable) requiring a minimum of 30 minutes of time, each 30 days." Average payment: $58.28.[28]

For a review of additional research on RPM, consult our earlier analysis in *The Transformative Power of Mobile Medicine*.[29]

Hospital at Home

For some healthcare providers, hospital at home may seem like an oxymoron; either patients are sick enough to justify hospital admission or they are well enough to receive home health services. But the economic forces currently facing healthcare have required more unconventional thinking. Research has demonstrated that hospital-at-home programs for patients with certain acute medical conditions can reduce complications and reduce the cost of care by 30% or more.[30] One of the most progressive programs to focus on this transition was spearheaded by Johns Hopkins Hospital in 1994. Bruce Leff, MD, and his colleagues have tested this program with 455 elderly patients from 3

Medicare-managed systems and a VA medical center.[31] They found that the home-care program met quality of care standards comparable to those expected of in-hospital programs. In addition, "On an intention-to-treat basis, patients treated in hospital-at-home had a shorter length of stay (3.2 vs. 4.9 days) (P = 0.004), and there was some evidence that they also had fewer complications. The mean cost was lower for hospital-at-home care than for acute hospital care ($5081 vs. $7480) ($P < 0.001$)."

Lesley Cryer and her colleagues at Presbyterian Healthcare Services in Albuquerque, NM, have demonstrated similar results when they put the Johns Hopkins model to work in their healthcare system.[32] They looked at over 500 patients in the program, which was limited to those in 9 diagnostic groups, including congestive heart failure, deep venous thrombosis, pneumonia, pulmonary embolism, complicated urinary tract infection, and dehydration. Patients had to live in a safe, stable environment and have basic utilities. Cryer et al. found that the home-care program was 19% less costly than a comparable inpatient group. The cost savings resulted primarily from a lower average length of stay and fewer lab and diagnostic tests. Patients also experienced comparable or better clinical outcomes and reported high-satisfaction levels.

Several other healthcare systems are now realizing the need to break free from overreliance on the hospital model of care, and a growing number of healthcare executives are looking to hospital-at-home models as delivery innovations. Steve Klasko, MD, CEO, of Thomas Jefferson University and Thomas Jefferson Health, for example, believes there is need for "a fundamental transformation from hospital care to 'health care with no address.' The goal is to deliver patients care how and where they consume everything else: at home or close to home via digital technologies."[33] The COVID-19 pandemic may foster greater interest in the hospital-at-home movement as the number of patients with life-threatening infections such as COVID-19 overwhelm hospitals around the world.

In the current healthcare environment, such programs present opportunities and challenges. Typically, candidates for this type of in-home acute care are chosen by ED physicians, who may have a list of specific conditions that are best suited for in-home care because there are clear-cut treatment protocols available to manage them. Congestive heart failure, chronic obstructive pulmonary disease, and community-acquired pneumonia fall into this category. As demonstrated in the Presbyterian Healthcare Services experiment, the patient's home also has to meet certain minimum requirements that ensure comfort, including air conditioning, heat, and running water.[30] These programs also need enough funding to pay for the biometric and communication devices required to monitor patients electronically. In the United States, such financial resources are limited because the CMS has yet to see the value of reimbursing clinicians for these services. Private insurers usually follow the federal government's position. On the other hand, several other countries are more willing to cover the cost of such innovative services.

Some hospital-at-home initiatives require daily visits by a physician, whereas others rely more heavily on telemedicine visits. Once again, financial considerations have to be kept in mind, since video conferencing requires that equipment be installed in the patient's home, and it requires high-speed Internet service to transmit data back and forth to the provider. Additional barriers to widespread adoption of this model include concerns among hospital clinicians and administrators about malpractice risks, should an inappropriate patient be entered into the program who subsequently develops complications, and the fact that hospitals may be reluctant to give up a hospital admission and the resulting loss of $10,000 to $12,000 of revenue per patient.

A meta-analysis of 61 randomized clinical trials that looked at hospital-at-home projects found that among 42 trials, which included almost 7,000 patients, this approach reduced mortality (odds ratio, 0.81). Similarly, they reduced readmission rates by 25% (odds ratio, 0.75), and lowered costs. The same analysis revealed that treating every 50 patients in such a program saved one life.[34]

Realizing the potential advantages of hospital-at-home programs, several large U.S. provider organizations have entered this space in the last few years, including Mayo Clinic, Partners Healthcare/Brigham and Women's Hospital, and Mount Sinai Health System in New York. Across the globe, there are also major programs in in Australia, South Wales, and Spain.

A case–control study that examined the Mount Sinai program, which included about 500 participants divided into 2 groups, found that patients in the hospital-at-home program experienced a shorter length of stay (3.2 days vs. 5.5 days), lower readmission rates (8.6% vs. 15.6%), fewer ED visits (5.8% vs. 11.7%), and greater patient satisfaction.[35] The study used a bundled payment system that included at-home services and a 30-day post-acute transitional care program. The better clinical outcomes observed in the home-care patients were accompanied by fewer adverse events, including fewer insertions of urinary catheters, which tend to be overused in a hospital setting and too often result in infections and death. Despite these positive findings, critics remain concerned about the lack of quality-of-care standards in this kind of setting. Hospitals, for instance, have to answer to The Joint Commission and require its certification to remain in business. No such national certifying body exists for hospital-at-home programs.

Partners Healthcare's hospital-at-home program has published strong evidence to support this approach to acute care. David Levine, MD, and his colleagues studied 91 patients in a randomized controlled trial (RCT). The 43 patients in the experimental group received nurse and physician home visits, as well as IV medications, remote monitoring, video visits, and point-of-care testing. The remaining patients received traditional hospital care.[36] The adjusted mean cost was 38% lower for hospital-at-home patients; they also had fewer laboratory test performed (median per admission 3 vs. 15), fewer imaging studies (14% vs. 44%), and fewer consultations (median 2% vs. 31%). The patients in the experimental program were also less sedentary and were readmitted to the hospital less often within 30 days (7% vs. 23%). Despite the reduced cost of care, hospital-at-home patients actually spent more time in the program, that is, length of stay was 4.5 versus 3.9 days. As was the case in other hospital-at-home patients, the Partners program had specific inclusion and exclusion criteria. "Participants were eligible for home hospital care if they resided within a 5-mile catchment area; had the capacity to consent (or could assent with the consent of a health care proxy who was physically present); were aged 18 years or older; and had a primary diagnosis of any infection, heart failure exacerbation, chronic obstructive pulmonary disease exacerbation, asthma exacerbation, or selected other conditions." Patients were not admitted into the program if they were in a long-term care or rehabilitation facility, needed routine administration

Figure 2.3 Mobile Devices Used by Advanced Care at Home Patients. (*Source:* Mayo Clinic Advanced Care at Home. Used with permission of Medically Home Group, Inc.)

(Information describing Figure 2.3 can be found on the following page.)

of a controlled substance, or "were considered to be at high risk for clinical deterioration on the basis of validated general and disease-specific risk algorithms."

In collaboration with a company called Medically Home, Mayo Clinic has developed a hospital-at-home program, which was initially launched in Florida. Similar to several other programs, it remotely monitors patients' vital signs. The program, officially called Advanced Care at Home, tracks heart rate, blood pressure, pulse oximetry, temperature, and respiratory rate. The devices are Bluetooth and connect to the Mayo/Medically Home system wirelessly. It also uses iPads, a battery back-up system from APC, and a Wi-Fi phone. (Devices used by patients in the Mayo system are illustrated in Figure 2.3.)

However, there are key differences between many home-care programs and the Mayo Clinic system. Many hospital-at-home programs are targeted and designed for low-acuity hospital patients, they use physician house calls as the clinical delivery model, and they have a short patient engagement period (2–4 days). The Medically Home affiliated setup is designed to handle an extended length of stay that includes acute, post-acute, and preventative care. It uses a scalable "decentralized" model for high-acuity care, and can manage a broad set of diverse use cases and support a large patient census. The program uses screening, training, contracting, quality management, and technology, and converts the currently "post-acute" community-based supply providers into "acute-level" providers, bringing goods and services to high-acuity patients at home while focusing heavily on the role of paramedics as the centerpiece of its ability to provide "rapid-response" capabilities. In practical terms, that means paramedics and other providers go into the home while being virtually connected with a centralized medical command center manned by physicians who guide the care for decentralized patients and the decentralized providers that care for patients.

The ideal patient population during the early stage of the program includes anyone sick enough to warrant being admitted to the hospital, while not being so sick to require intensive care, invasive procedures, or advanced imaging. On any given day, the program has several patients in-house with congestive heart failure, pneumonia, cellulitis, and an array of other conditions which require that patients receive routine labs, medication therapy, monitoring and medical intervention to ensure appropriate adjustments to the care plan. Additional disease states that may qualify, depending on each patient's status, include bronchitis with asthma, fever accompanying gastroenteritis, hypovolemia, pancreatitis, renal failure, respiratory failure, urinary tract infection, and deep vein thrombosis. Before patients are admitted to Advanced Care at Home, the care team evaluates the home environment to ensure that they have running water, electricity, Wi-Fi and/or cell service, and depending on the diagnosis/acuity–caregiver support. A more detailed description that illustrates how the program

What is the advanced care at home model?

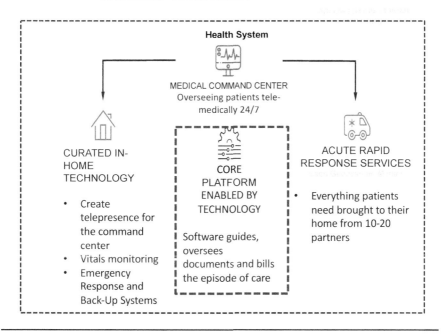

Health System

MEDICAL COMMAND CENTER
Overseeing patients tele-
medically 24/7

CURATED IN-
HOME
TECHNOLOGY

- Create
  telepresence for
  the command
  center
- Vitals monitoring
- Emergency
  Response and
  Back-Up Systems

CORE
PLATFORM
ENABLED BY
TECHNOLOGY

Software guides,
oversees
documents and bills
the episode of care

ACUTE RAPID
RESPONSE SERVICES

- Everything patients
  need brought to their
  home from 10-20
  partners

Figure 2.4   Advanced Care at Home, administered by Medically Home Group, Inc., is coordinated through a medical command center that is manned 24/7 and employs an acute rapid response team, telemedicine services, and numerous remote patient monitoring devices. (*Source:* Mayo Clinic Advanced Care at Home. Used with permission of Medically Home Group, Inc.)

is administrated, along with a graphic explanation of the supplier ecosystem, see Figures 2.4 and 2.5.

Telemedicine, remote patient monitoring, and home-care programs have been in existence for decades, but new technologies and the advent of the COVID-19 pandemic have presented new opportunities and new challenges that are being met by healthcare providers with the willingness to question the status quo. Although some providers and vendors still offer poor quality patient care, controlled clinical research is slowly generating the evidence to distinguish high-quality care from poor-quality care.

Advanced Care at Home Supplier Ecosystem

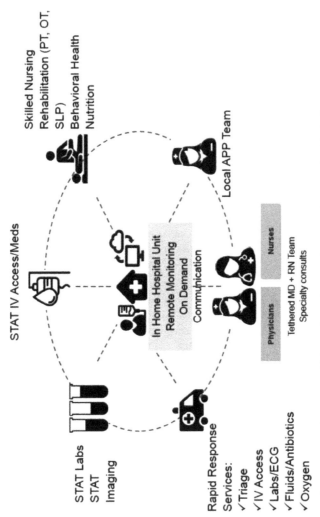

Replicating the capabilities of a brick and mortar hospital with in-home services

Figure 2.5 The home care program provides a constant supply of resources as needed, including physicians, registered nurses, physical therapists, IV services, stat labs, and much more. (*Source:* Mayo Clinic Advanced Care at Home. Used with permission of Medically Home Group, Inc.)

References

1. Mann DM, Chen J, Chunara R, et al. COVID-19 transforms health care through telemedicine: evidence from the field. *JAMIA*. May 29, 2020. https://doi.org/10.1093/jamia/ocaa072

2. Federation of State Medical Boards. U.S. states and territories modifying requirements in response to COVID 19. May 26, 2020. https://www.fsmb.org/siteassets/advocacy/pdf/states-waiving-licensure-requirements-for-telehealth-in-response-to-covid-19.pdf

3. American Medical Association. Advocacy Resource Center: telemedicine. April 27, 2020. https://www.ama-assn.org/system/files/2020-04/telemedicine-state-orders-directives-chart.pdf

4. American Telemedicine Association. CMS interim final rule: summary of key telehealth provisions. May 1, 2020. https://www.americantelemed.org/policies/cms-interim-final-rule-summary-of-key-telehealth-provisions/

5. Department of Health and Human Services. Medicare and Medicaid Programs, Basic Health Program, and Exchanges; Additional Policy and Regulatory Revisions in Response to the COVID-19 Public Health Emergency and Delay of Certain Reporting Requirements for the Skilled Nursing Facility Quality Reporting Program. April 30, 2020. https://www.cms.gov/files/document/covid-medicare-and-medicaid-ifc2.pdf

6. Bestsennyy, O, Gilbert C, Harris A, Rost J. Telehealth: a quarter-trillion-dollar post-COVID-19 reality? McKinsey & Company. May 2020. https://www.mckinsey.com/~/media/McKinsey/Industries/Healthcare%20Systems%20and%20Services/Our%20Insights/Telehealth%20A%20quarter%20trillion%20dollar%20post%20COVID%2019%20reality/Telehealth-A-quarter-trillion dollar-post-COVID-19-reality.ashx

7. ACOG Committee Opinion # 798. Implementing telehealth in practice. *Obstetrics Gyncol.* 2020; 135:e73–e79.

8. League J, Angers J, Daugherty A. How Covid-19 will impact telehealth. June 3, 2020. https://www.advisory.com/research/health-care-it-advisor/expert-insights/2020/how-covid-19-will-impact-telehealth

9. Trzcinski A. The Forrester New Wave™: virtual care solutions for digital health, Q2 2019. June 5, 2019. https://interactive.healthleadersmedia.com/VirtualCare Solutions

10. American Medical Association. *Telehealth Implementation Playbook.* 2020. https://www.ama-assn.org/system/files/2020-04/ama-telehealth-playbook.pdf

11. Wild S, Hanley J, Lewis SC, et al. Supported telemonitoring and glycemic control in people with type 2 diabetes: the Telescot diabetes pragmatic multicenter randomized controlled trial. *PLoS Med.* 2016. Available from http://journals.plos.org/plosmedicine/article?id510.1371/journal.pmed.1002098.

12. Resneck JS, Abrouk M, Steuer M, et al. Choice, transparency, coordination, and quality among direct-to-consumer telemedicine websites and apps treating skin disease. *JAMA Dermatol.* 2016;152:76875.

13. Schoenfeld AJ, Davies JM, Marafino BJ, et al. Variation in quality of care provided during commercial virtual visits in urgent care: a standardized patient audit study. *JAMA Intern Med.* 2016;176:635–642.

14. Haimi M, Brammli-Greeberg S, Baron-Epel O, Waisman Y. Assessing patient safety in a pediatric telemedicine setting: a multi-methods study. *BMC Medical Informatics and Decision Making.* 2020;20:63.

15. Arora S, Thornton K, Murata G, et al. Outcomes of treatment for hepatitis C virus infection by primary care providers. *N Engl J Med.* 2011;364:2199–2207.

16. Jain T, Lu RJ, Mehrotra A. Prescriptions on demand: the growth of direct-to-consumer telemedicine companies. *JAMA.* 2019;322:925–926.

17. Oksman E, Linna M, Horhammer I, et al. Cost-effectiveness analysis for a tele-based health coaching program for chronic disease in primary care. *BMC Health Services Res.* 2017;17:138.

18. Kim J-H, Desai E, Cole MB. How the rapid shift to telehealth leaves many community health centers behind during the COVID-19 pandemic. *Health Affairs Blog.* June 2, 2020.

19. Bavafa H, Hitt LM, Terwiech C. The impact of e-visits on visit frequencies and patient health: evidence from primary care. *SSRN.* July 22, 2017. https://papers.ssrn.com/sol3/papers.cfm?abstract_id=2363705

20. Ashwood JS, Mehrotra A, Cowling D, et al. Direct-to-consumer telehealth may increase access to care but does not decrease spending. *Health Affairs.* 2017;36:485–491.

21. Black Hat. The 2020 Black Hat USA attendee survey, *Cyber Threats in Turbulent Times.* June 2020. https://i.blackhat.com/docs/usa/2020/P3_28203_BH20_Report.pdf?elq_mid=1640&elq_cid=3670712

22. Jercich K. COVID-19-triggered threat changes will linger beyond crisis, say most security pros. *Healthcare IT News.* June 25, 2020. https://www.healthcareitnews.com/news/covid-19-triggered-threat-changes-will-linger-beyond-crisis-say-most-security-pros?utm_source=SFMC&utm_medium=email&utm_campaign=NL-HITN-NewsWeek-2020-06-30-Theme+Month%E2%80%8B

23. Van Sickle D, Magzamen S, Truelove S, Morrison T. Remote monitoring of inhaled bronchodilator use and weekly feedback about asthma management: an open-group, short-term pilot study of the impact on asthma control. *PLOS ONE.* 2013;8:e55335.

24. Kvedar JC, Colman C, Cella G. *The Internet of Healthy Things.* Boston, MA: Partners Connected Health; 2015;38.

25. Fan KG, Mandel J, Agnihotri P, et al. Remote patient monitoring technologies for predicting chronic obstructive pulmonary disease exacerbations: review and comparison. *JMIR MHealth and UHealth.* 2020;8:e16147.

26. Abel R. Remote patient monitoring case study. HomeHealth Visiting Nurses. Maine Health. https://netrc.org/wp-content/uploads/2015/10/Panel-3-RPM-HHVN-Abel.pdf. Accessed July 6, 2020.

27. Jeong IC, Healy R, Bao B, et al. Assessment of patient ambulation profiles to predict hospital readmission, discharge location, and length of stay in a cardiac surgery

progressive care unit. *JAMA Network Open*. 2020;3(3):e201074. doi: 10.1001 /jamanetworkopen.2020.1074

28. Propeller Staff. Your guide to the new CPT codes for remote patient monitoring (RPM). Propeller, April 9, 2019. https://www.propellerhealth.com/press/ clinical-blog/your-guide-to-the-new-cpt-codes-for-remote-patient-monitoring/

29. Cerrato, P, Halamka J. *The Transformative Power of Mobile Medicine*. Cambridge, MA: Elsevier/Academic Press; 2019.

30. Klein S. "Hospital at home" programs improve outcomes, lower costs but face resistance from providers and payers. *The Commonwealth Fund*. https://www .commonwealthfund.org/publications/newsletter-article/hospital-home-programs -improve-outcomes-lower-costs-face-resistance. Accessed January 15, 2020.

31. Leff B, Burton L, Mader SL, et al. Hospital at home: feasibility and outcomes of a program to provide hospital-level care at home for acutely ill older patients. *Ann Intern Med*. 2005;143:798–808.

32. Cryer L, Shannon SB, Van Amsterdam M, Leff B. Costs for "hospital at home" patients were 19 percent lower, with equal or better outcomes compared to similar inpatients. *Health Affairs*. 2012;31:1237–1243.

33. Sullivan T. Top CEO priorities for the next 3–5 years. *Health Evolution*. January 3, 2020. https://www.healthevolution.com/insider/top-ceo-priorities-for-the-next-3 -5-years/#new-entrants

34. Caplan GA, Sulaiman NS, Mangin DA, et al. A meta-analysis of "hospital in the home." *Med J Aust*. 2012;197:512–519.

35. Federman AD, Soones T, DeCherrie LV, et al. Association of a bundled hospital-at-home and 30-day postacute transitional care program with clinical outcomes and patient experiences. *JAMA Intern Med*. 2018;178:1033–1040.

36. Levine DM, Ouchi K, Blanchfield B, et al. Hospital-level care at home for acutely ill adults: a randomized controlled trial. *Ann Intern Med*. 2020;172(2):77–85.

Chapter 3

The Digital Assault on COVID-19

The adage that warns, "Those who ignore history are destined to repeat it," certainly applies to the COVID-19 pandemic. The Spanish Flu pandemic of 1918 and the 20th century emergence of pellagra, a nutritional disease, both have lessons worth remembering in this context.

The 1918 pandemic, which killed as many as 50 to 100 million people, generated a xenophobic epidemic against Germans, Italians, and Chinese, not unlike the current social and political climate in which China has been blamed for the spread of COVID-19 around the globe. The flu pandemic also called into question the credibility of the scientific and medical establishments of its day, which, in turn, led to newfound interest in alternative medicine, back to nature movements, spiritualism, and all sorts of "cures."[1] Similarly, in 1918, "tensions arose over the interests of communities versus individuals," not unlike the tensions that currently exist in many U.S. states in which critics of face masks, social distancing, and business lockdowns complain that their individual freedoms are being restricted and their right to earn a living is being thwarted. Laura Spinney, author of *Pale Rider: The Spanish Flu and How It Changed the World*,[2] has also documented the psychological shift towards pessimism, irony, and absurdity during that period in history, also mirroring what many are experiencing as they live through the current crisis.

Similarly, in the early 1900s, the emergence of pellagra in the southern United States created a "culture war" of its own. Dr. Joseph Goldberger demonstrated that the signposts for the disease—dermatitis, dementia, and diarrhea—resulted from a vitamin B3 (niacin) deficiency, which, in turn, was linked to poverty and a corn-based diet. That indisputable truth was disputed for decades by many Southern citizens and politicians, who insisted that it was a story contrived by Northerners to denigrate Southern culture. The end result was many lost lives, much like the lost lives from COVID-19 that have resulted from inaction in many countries, coupled with an anti-science, anti-expertise mindset.

The digital transformation of healthcare that serves as the theme of this book does not directly address the social and cultural issues mentioned above, but a review of the latest developments in data science, predictive analytics, and machine learning (ML) will nonetheless help alleviate some of the suffering that the pandemic has caused.

Developing Better Predictive and Diagnostic Tools

Researchers have been developing promising patient assessment protocols and diagnostic tools that incorporate artificial intelligence (AI), convolutional neural networks (CNNs), CT scans, and patients' signs and symptoms. Mei et al. have evaluated a digital platform that involved 3 AI models to estimate the probability that a patient will become COVID-19 positive. One relies on a chest CT scan; another on clinical data, including temperature, exposure to the virus, presence of fever and cough, and white blood cell count; and a third combines the CT scan with the clinical data.[3] Initially, the investigators created a CNN to recognize the distinct features of COVID-19 in a CT scan. Using patients' clinical data, they subsequently used a support vector machine (SVM), random forest analysis, and multilayer perception classifiers (MLPs) to classify COVID-19 patients and found that MLP was the most useful AI tool. Then they combined CT and clinical data in a second neural network to predict each patient's COVID status. They evaluated 905 patients that had already been tested with RT-PCR, of whom 46.3% tested positive for COVID-19. Using a test dataset of 279 patients, the AI system that combined CT scans and clinical data generated an Area Under the Curve (AUC) of 0.92 and was as sensitive as the findings of a senior thoracic radiologist in detecting the infection.

Kang Zhang, with the Macau University of Science and Technology (Macau, China), and associates have likewise developed an AI system to help diagnose COVID-19. In addition, their algorithms predicted whether a patient will progress into what they refer to as novel coronavirus pneumonia (NCP).[4] Using a large dataset of CT scans and clinical parameters, they created an AI system to differentiate between NCP and other types of infectious pneumonia, employing both retrospective and prospective trial designs. Their system was accurate in both case-dense areas like Wuhan, non-epidemic regions like Hafei, and in Ecuador. COVID-19 CT-detected lesions were also correlated with specific clinical parameters: "C-reactive protein (CRP), age, serum lactic dehydrogenase (LDH), highest body temperature (Tmax), and neutrophil-to-lymphocyte ratio showed highly positive correlations with the lesion features. By contrast, degree of blood oxygen saturation, lymphocyte count, albumin, blood platelets, and Na+ showed highly negative correlations with the lesion features."

Although Mei et al. and Zhang et al. have devised creative approaches to detecting the presence or severity of COVID-19, their protocols only evaluate traditional parameters, namely, CT scans, clinical data, and lab values. Proteomic and metabolomic analyses of COVID-19 patients' sera employ a more "out-of-the-box" approach, an approach that suggests the existence of several new predictive markers. For instance, Bo Shen and his colleagues[5] profiled 46 COVID-19 patients and 53 controls to look for distinctive proteins and metabolites that may help distinguish patients with severe infection from those without the disease and those with mild infection. Once these markers were identified, Shen et al. used ML (random forest modeling) to detect molecular changes in patients with severe COVID-19 that implicated "dysregulation of macrophage, platelet degranulation, complement system pathways, and massive metabolic suppression." The researchers were able to predict the progression to severe infection based on the expression levels of 22 serum proteins and 7 metabolites. Among the proteins linked to severe COVID-19 were serum amyloid A1 and A2, C-reactive protein, and acute phase proteins such as alpha-1-antichymotrypsin (SERPINA3). The analysis also found elevated levels of certain molecules associated with hepatic damage, including elevated glucose, glucuronate, bilirubin degradation product, and several bile acid derivatives.

There are also digital tools designed to help make an early diagnosis of COVID-19 by analyzing electronic health records (EHRs). A Mayo Clinic platform that included over 77,000 patients who underwent PCR testing for COVID-19 were evaluated using transformer neural networks on unstructured clinical notes. The analysis revealed previously unrecognized early signs and symptoms of COVID-19. In the past, clinicians were warning the public to look for cough, fever, and difficult breathing as the signposts for infection. The analysis conducted by Wagner et al. identified anosmia and dysgeusia in patients a week before they tested positive for the infection.[6] COVID-19-positive patients were more than 27 times as likely to present with impaired smell and taste, when compared to COVID-19 negative patients. By comparison, the presence of fever/chills, cough, and respiratory difficulty occurred about twice as often in positive versus negative patients.

Several groups are attempting to estimate a person's risk of the infection or the likelihood that it will cause life-threatening complications. Johns Hopkins and University of Maryland researchers have constructed a digital COVID-19 risk calculator to help individualize the likelihood of a person dying from the infection.[7] It is based on an analysis using sociodemographic factors and pre-existing conditions in the U.S. population. When the model used to create the calculator was tested across 477 U.S. cities and a Medicare population age 65 and older, Jin et al. concluded: "Projections show that the model can identify relatively small fractions of the population (for example 4.3%) that might experience a disproportionately large number of deaths (for example 48.7%), but there is wide variation in risk across communities."[8] The calculator asks for a person's age, zip code, race or ethnic group, sex, height and weight, smoking history, and history of asthma, other chronic respiratory disorders, chronic heart disease, diabetes, cancer, stroke, rheumatoid arthritis, systemic lupus, or psoriasis, hypertension, or chronic kidney disease. Once this data is entered into the calculator, it generates a risk score and risk category, ranging from close to or lower-than-average risk to very high risk.

A wider search of the literature on COVID-19 predictive tools has not been as encouraging, however. One analysis evaluated 145 predictive models and concluded that they were all poorly reported and likely biased.[9] A second analysis that tested 22 prognostic models on 411 patients with COVID-19 was likewise unimpressive. It found they were no more useful than oxygen saturation readings at room air for predicting clinical deterioration.[10] Knowing a patient's age was just as predictive of mortality.

On a more positive note, the recently developed 4C Deterioration model has proven more robust for the management of COVID-19. It was tested prospectively using a multi-center database of consecutive patients, with more than 66,000 patients used to develop the model and 8,000 to externally validate it.[11] It has proven reliable in 260 hospitals in 9 National Health Service regions in England, Wales, and Scotland. Reviewers concluded that "[t]he careful analysis and good results from external validation suggest that the 4C Deterioration model could be used to support clinicians in the decision to keep a patient in the hospital, admit a patient to critical care, or initiate therapy."[9] The predictive tool used 11 commonly available markers to identify at-risk patients: age, C-reactive protein, lymphocyte count, respiratory rate, oxygen saturation, urea concentration, Glasgow coma scale, the presence of nosocomial infection, sex, room air of oxygen, and radiographic infiltrates.

Predictive models not only have the potential to detect infection in individual patients but also the ability to help manage the pandemic at the population level by forecasting when infection surges are likely to occur in various regions of a country. In the past, Google attempted to detect increases in the incidence of influenza with its Flu Trends algorithm. Although that initiative was unsuccessful, combining data from Google, Twitter, UpToDate, and de-identified mobility data from smartphones is showing promise.[12] In a yet-to-be-peer-reviewed international study led by Harvard University investigators, several digital data streams were analyzed to see if they might help predict both increases and decreases in COVID-19 case counts over time. Several sources were used: social network microblogs from Twitter, Internet searches, point-of-care medical software (UpToDate), GLEAM, a metapopulation mechanistic model, anonymized and aggregated human mobility data from smartphones, and Smart Thermometer measurements. Kogan et al. found: "exponential growth roughly 2–3 weeks prior to comparable growth in confirmed COVID-19 cases and 3–4 weeks prior to comparable growth in COVID-19 deaths across the US over the last 6 months." They also observed "exponential decay in confirmed cases and deaths 5–6 weeks after implementation of NPIs [nonpharmaceutical interventions], as measured by anonymized and aggregated human mobility data from mobile phones."

Growing the Knowledge Base

Predictive tools that help pinpoint those at risk of COVID-19 and its complications are not the only applications for AI and ML. The search for effective vaccines, treatments, and diagnostic tools depends on an effective knowledge base, and in this arena, AI and ML are likewise playing an important role. An entire subspecialty of bioscience has evolved that focuses on the development of knowledge graphs that help scientists conceptualize and construct pathophysiologic pathways, which can then lead to finding new drug and vaccine candidates to defeat infectious diseases. Several of these initiatives are now directed toward understanding how the coronavirus enters human cells and how it affects the immune system.

A recent example of this is the early research on baricitinib, a Janus kinase inhibitor. Combining our knowledge of the 2019-nCoV virus, molecular modeling, and an ML-enhanced search of the scientific literature, it was possible to construct a knowledge graph that suggested the drug might have a therapeutic effect on COVID-19.[13] Since that graph was published in February 2020, clinical research has confirmed the agent's value, leading up to the FDA's emergency use authorization of baricitinib (Olumiant) for the treatment of COVID-19: "Baricitinib is approved by the Food and Drug Administration (FDA) to treat moderate to severe rheumatoid arthritis. On November 19, 2020, the FDA issued an Emergency Use Authorization (EUA) for the use of baricitinib in combination with remdesivir in hospitalized adults and children aged ≥2 years with COVID-19 who require supplemental oxygen, invasive mechanical ventilation, or extracorporeal membrane oxygenation (ECMO)."[14]

Similarly, nference, a data analytics company, uses a digital engine called nferX to compile intelligence that will likely advance our understanding of the virus. nferX is a biomedical knowledge synthesis platform that is being deployed in partnership with Mayo Clinic to better understand how SARS-CoV-2 evades the human immune system and exploits host cellular responses to get a foothold. nference reported its finding about how SARS-CoV-2 has evolved a unique spike protein cleavage site that is identical to the proteolytic site present in an ancient sodium channel (ENaC-α). This finding suggests that SARSCoV-2, but not previous coronavirus strains, performs targeted molecular mimicry of ENaC-α, a protein with extensive genetic evidence of aldosterone dysregulation.[15] A separate study was the first to map the viral receptor (ACE2) at unprecedented scale and resolution. This study revealed the gastrointestinal (GI) system and the cardiovascular-renal system as salient foci for COVID-19 pathogenesis beyond the respiratory system.[16]

A Holistic Approach to the Pandemic

ML–based algorithms also suggest that viral/host interactions play an important role in determining which individuals become infected. That realization is certainly no surprise to clinicians who have known for decades that the risk of contracting most infections depends on the virulence, concentration, and exposure to the microbe on the one hand and the resilience of the human host on the other. The latter, in turn, is dependent on a person's nutritional status, the presence of co-existing disease, their weight—obesity and malnutrition are both risk factors—and a list of other co-factors. In a recent review published in Mayo Clinic Proceedings: Innovations, Quality, and Outcomes, we discuss these interactions at length.[17]

In that review, we also discuss the value of network medicine and systems biology in revealing which of these co-factors are most relevant in the search for the best preventive strategy. Currently, the most effective way to prevent COVID-19 is through social distancing, protective gear such as face masks and respirators, and vaccines. But over time, addressing several other risk factors, including diet, stress, single-nucleotide polymorphisms, and environmental toxins such as air pollution and firsthand and secondhand tobacco smoke will likely play an equally important role: "Employing machine learning-enhanced algorithms to analyze all the aforementioned risk factors and their interactions may help determine which ones predict a patient's risk of COVID-19 or the prognosis of someone who has already tested positive."[17]

The Institute for Integrative Health has taken a similar holistic approach to patient care for the U.S. military, taking advantage of the landmark research conducted by Herbert Benson, MD, from Massachusetts General Hospital and his colleagues. Between 2001 and 2017, the U.S. Armed Forces developed several holistic treatment approaches under an umbrella initiative called the Epidaurus Project.[18] The project took advantage of the healing abilities of nature, spirituality, and the arts to treat post-traumatic stress disorder (PTSD) and traumatic brain injury among soldiers who had not responded to conventional therapies.

Foote et al. emphasize the same shortcomings of the conventional approach to healthcare that we have discussed in previous publications, namely, the fact that reductionistic thinking has "difficulty when attempting to conceptualize 'whole person' issues, including personal suffering, overall wellness/ill health, and public health concerns. . . . Holism, the effort to know the body as a total entity, maintains this concept at center stage." The holistic modalities used at Walter Reed Army Medical Center (WRAMC) have included building designs that immerse patients in a healing environment, family-centered care, multidisciplinary care integration, and a variety of basic wellness services that include nutrition; exercise; stress management; the use of music, visual art, and related creative arts; and complementary medicine.

Criticisms of this approach to patient care and claims of its "unscientific" nature have centered around its inability to generate metrics that quantitatively document the therapeutic value of these unconventional therapies. The Epidaurus 2 project addressed this problem by developing metrics that focused on genomics, integrated biometrics that record physiological changes caused by the stress response, and ML. With natural language processing, for instance, clinicians were able to identify certain speech patterns associated with post-traumatic stress. Similarly, researchers have found content word analysis that incorporated by NLP and ML could differentiate between authentic suicide notes and elicited notes written by healthy controls. Will such modalities have a role to play in the treatment of COVID-19? We suspect they will.

The COVID-19 Healthcare Coalition

Few initiatives have had as much impact on the pandemic as the COVID-19 Healthcare Coalition, a collaboration among healthcare organizations, technology vendors, academicians, non-profit groups, and startups. Launched in March 2020, the Coalition initially concentrated on providing personal protective equipment (PPE) for healthcare workers. It also helped develop the infrastructure required to make collaboration a reality and to share analytics. More specifically, it "identified quality manufacturing sources, negotiated low prices, worked around numerous export challenges, and were able to deliver 675,000 masks to over 60 locations during a time when 50% of hospitals in New York

City were running out of N95 respirators. Through the partnership of the charity Masks4America, these masks went to hotspots including Illinois, Virginia, Maryland, Louisiana, Michigan, Washington, DC, and Puerto Rico. The Coalition also helped to accelerate production of 10,000 low cost ventilators, and aggregated a marketplace catalog to provide buyers the simplest possible access to the many PPE marketplaces that have emerged across the country."

Early in the pandemic, PPE was in short supply, which promoted the group to recruit INPRO Technologies to develop an ultraviolet germicidal irradiation design to help safely recycle used equipment. Several members of the Coalition, including Cardinal Health, GHX, LLamasoft, LogicStream Health, MITRE, and Sodexo Healthcare Services, also developed a PPE and pharmaceuticals demand model to help state and local leaders determine if their PPE stock was adequate to meet expected demand.

As we go to press, 2 COVID-19 vaccines have been authorized by the U.S. FDA for emergency use—the Pfizer-BioNTech and the Moderna products. Others are in the pipeline. Several initiatives are now underway to provide individuals with some sort of "vaccination passport" that they can store on a smartphone to prove they have received the COVID-19 vaccine. Nonetheless, we want to empower patients with tools that support whatever choices they make.

COVID-19 may be the most horrific pandemic since the 1918 flu, but it can also serve as an opportunity to rewrite the future of the human race—on so many levels. It can be the steppingstone to a reimagined economy, a more equitable healthcare ecosystem, a more productive workforce, and a cleaner planet. These eventualities will result from several phenomena that have transpired since the start of the pandemic. They include a distributed workforce that resulted from the need to remain socially distant, the increased acceptance of telemedicine, the significant drop in air and water pollution precipitated by fewer motorists on the roads and less factory output, and much more. In the words of Jack Hidary, a technology researcher and entrepreneur: "We can rewire our economy as we reopen it. We can leapfrog to a better structure instead of reverting to the old way."[19]

References

1. Horton R. Offline: Covid-19—what we can expect to come. *Lancet.* 2020; 395(10240):1821.
2. Spinney L. *Pale Rider: The Spanish Flu of 1918 and How It Changed the World.* New York, NY: Hachette Books; 2017.
3. Mei X, Lee H-C, Diao K-Y, et al. Artificial intelligence–enabled rapid diagnosis of patients with COVID-19. *Nat Med.* 2020. https://doi.org/10.1038/s41591-020-0931-3

4. Zhang K, Liu X, Shen J, et al. Clinically applicable AI system for accurate diagnosis, quantitative measurements, and prognosis of COVID-19 pneumonia using computed tomography. *Cell.* 2020;181(6):1423–1433.

5. Shen B, Yi X, Sun Y, et al. Proteomic and metabolomic characterization of COVID-19 patient sera. *Cell.* https://doi.org/10.1016/j.cell.2020.05.032

6. Wagner T, Shweta F, Murugadoss K, et al. Augmented curation of clinical notes from a massive EHR system reveals symptoms of impending COVID-19 diagnosis. *eLife.* 2020 Jul 7;9:e58227. doi: 10.7554/eLife.58227.

7. Williamson EJ, Walker AJ, Bhaskara K, et al. Factors associated with COVID-19-related death using OpenSAFELY. *Nature.* 2020;584:431–439.

8. Jin J, Agarwala N, Kundu P, et al. Individual and community-level risk for COVID-19 mortality in the United States. *Nat Med.* 2020. https://doi.org/10.1038/s41591-020-01191-8

9. Wynants L, Sotgiu G. Improving clinical management of COVID-19: the role of prediction models. *Lancet Respir Med.* Published online: January 11, 2021. https://www.thelancet.com/journals/lanres/article/PIIS2213-2600(21)00006-0/fulltext

10. Gupta RK, Marks M, Samuels HA, et al. Systematic evaluation and external validation of 22 prognostic models among hospitalised adults with COVID-19: an observational cohort study. *Eur Respir J.* 2020;56(6):2003498. https://doi.org/10.1183/13993003.03498-2020

11. Gupta RK, Harrison EM, Ho A, et al. Development and validation of the ISARIC 4C deterioration model for adults hospitalised with COVID-19: a prospective cohort study. *Lancet Respir Med.* 2021. Published online: January 11, 2021. https://doi.org/10.1016/S2213-2600(20)30559-2

12. Kogan NE, Clemente L, Liautaud P, et al. An early warning approach to monitor COVID-19 activity with multiple digital traces in near real-time. arXiv.org > stat > arXiv:2007.00756

13. Richardson P, Griffin I, Tucker C, et al. Baricitinib as potential treatment for 2019-nCoV acute respiratory disease. *Lancet.* Published online: February 4, 2020. https://www.thelancet.com/journals/lancet/article/PIIS0140-6736(20)30304-4/fulltext

14. National Institutes of Health. COVID 19 treatment guidelines. The COVID-19 Treatment Guidelines Panel's Statement on the Emergency Use Authorization of Baricitinib for the Treatment of COVID-19. December 14, 2020. https://www.covid19treatmentguidelines.nih.gov/statement-on-baricitinib-eua/

15. Anand P, Puranik A, Aravamudan M, et al. SARS-CoV-2 selectively mimics a cleavable peptide of human ENaC in a strategic hijack of host proteolytic machinery. *eLife.* 2020;9:e58603. doi: 10.7554/eLife.58603

16. Venkatakrishnan A, Puranik A, Anand A, et al. Knowledge synthesis of 100 million biomedical documents augments the deep expression profiling of coronavirus receptors. *eLife.* 2020;9:e58040. doi: 10.7554/eLife.58040

17. Halamka J, Cerrato, P, Perlman A. Redesigning COVID-19 care with network medicine and machine learning. *Mayo Clin Proc Innov Qual Outcomes.* 2020; 4:725–732. https://pubmed.ncbi.nlm.nih.gov/33043272/

18. Foote RP, Benson H, Berger A, et al. Advanced metrics for assessing holistic care: the "Epidaurus 2" Project. *Global Adv Health Med.* 2018;7:1–19. doi: 10.1177/2164957X18755981

19. *Return to a Smarter Economy with Jack Hidary.* YouTube. May 1, 2020. https://www.youtube.com/watch?v=IfVBcLWH0q4. Accessed January 31, 2021.

Chapter 4

Entering the Age of Big Data and AI-Assisted Medicine

There are rare moments in history when technology, policy, and urgency to change converge—"a perfect storm of innovation." This is one of those moments. This may sound overly optimistic to many healthcare professionals and technologists, but this vision is not naivete but *evidence-based* optimism. The realization of this vision is being accelerated by the COVID-19 pandemic, but there are many other drivers pushing it forward, including recent advances in clinical medicine, care coordination, and patient engagement, partnerships with major technology companies, as well as innovations in machine learning (ML) and data analytics. The end result will be: "More cures. Earlier diagnoses. Treatments tailored to each person at a precise moment. Healthier populations. The scourge of potential pandemics eradicated just as they emerge."[1]

The role of artificial intelligence (AI) in this future is playing out in a wide array of clinical areas, including gastroenterology, mental health, pathology, cancer diagnosis, critical care medicine, endocrinology, and pharmacology. It is being enabled with the help of several digital tools, including convolutional neural networks, clustering, random forest modeling, and gradient boosting.

Diabetes

In the field of data analytics, predictive algorithms have received much of the attention because of their ability to forecast which patients are most likely to progress from preclinical to clinical disease and to forewarn clinicians about patients most likely to convert from mild symptomatology to life-threatening complications. The American Diabetes Association (ADA) has been advising health professionals and patients for several years about the danger of prediabetes. Unfortunately, too few are taking these warnings seriously enough. ADA defines prediabetes as fasting plasma glucose between 100 and 126 mg/dl, a 2-hour oral glucose tolerance test reading between 140 and 200 mg/dl, or hemoglobin A1c of 5.7% to 6.5%.[2] The Association has developed a risk assessment tool to help clinicians and patients; it asks for a patient's age, gender, family history of diabetes, the presence of hypertension, whether the patient is physically active, their ethnicity, and height and weight. Although this kind of scoring system will detect many persons with prediabetes, it has its limitations and ignores many of the changes in a patient's medical history over time. An AI-enabled assessment tool that takes advantage of gradient boosting, on the other hand, is capable of factoring many more risk factors gleaned from a patient's electronic health record. This type of assessment system can accurately predict which patients will progress to full-blown diabetes, with an area under the curve (AUC) of 0.865.[3] The gradient boosting approach has proven more accurate than logistic regression and evaluation of standard clinical cutoffs of blood glucose $\geq$ 110 mg/dl and HbA1c $\geq$ 6.0%. Cahn et al.'s evaluation of said ML algorithm incorporated 69 variables to achieve its superior AUC.

There is also reason to believe that AI-enhanced algorithms can help identify individuals before they become prediabetic. The Centers for Disease Control and Prevention (CDC) has a screening test to help predict prediabetes that asks one's age, family history of diabetes, the existence of hypertension, race or ethnicity, whether one is physically active, gender, height, and weight. But logistic regression, artificial neural networks, random forest analysis, and gradient boosting have been demonstrated to uncover numerous other risk factors to help predict prediabetes. Among the predictors that may help refine the risk stratification process: food security, citizenship, monocyte count, uric acid level, ALT, RBC count, and serum calcium and potassium.[4] Whereas the CDC screening tool returned an area under the receiver operating characteristic (AUROC) of 64.4% in a large cohort from the National Health and Nutrition Survey, several AI-based algorithms generated AUROCs at or above 70%.

Cardiovascular Disease

ML-based solutions are making significant inroads in cardiovascular disease. FDA-approved single-lead mobile EKG systems have been available for several years and are well supported by research. A 6-lead mobile EKG has received approval by the agency as well. Both have successfully been used to meet the challenge of diagnosing and monitoring atrial fibrillation. ML-assisted algorithms are also showing promise in meeting the challenge of correctly diagnosing heart failure (HF). Currently, the diagnosis is made by evaluating a patient's ejection fraction, a measure of how much blood leaves the heart with each contraction. Patients with HF are divided into 3 broad categories: reduced ejection fraction, mid-range injection fraction, and preserved injection fraction. But even HF specialists have trouble making the diagnosis. In addition to ejection fraction, there are several other factors that need to be taken into account when making the determination, including shortness of breath, ankle swelling, poor exercise tolerance, a history of coronary artery disease and hypertension, EKG readings, left ventricular mass index, and tricuspid regurgitation velocity. Using ML to analyze a large assortment of risk factors and large data set of patients can help clinicians improve the likelihood of detecting the condition. South Korean investigators performed a retrospective analysis of over 1,100 patients with and without HF using random forest modeling, decision tree, and several other tools and found that classification and a regression tree were most accurate in predicting HF.[5] When Choi et al. combined the results of their ML analysis with a knowledge base they derived from clinical guidelines, a literature search, and the resultant clinical knowledge decision tree, they generated a hybrid algorithm (Figure 4.1) that they then tested prospectively. Their conclusion: "In a prospective pilot study of 97 patients presenting with dyspnea to the outpatient clinic, 44% had heart failure. The concordance rate between AI-CDSS [AI-assisted clinical decision support system] and heart failure specialists was 98%, whereas that between non-heart failure specialists and heart failure specialists was 76%. In conclusion, AI-CDSS showed a high diagnostic accuracy for heart failure. Therefore, AI-CDSS may be useful for the diagnosis of heart failure, especially when heart failure specialists are not available." The prospective nature of the Choi et al. study sets it apart from the many AI-related investigations that have relied solely on retrospective analysis. One should also bear in mind, however, that the prospective arm only included 97 patients.

Machine learning is also helping to improve the interpretation of echocardiograms, the most widely used imaging approach to evaluate cardiac function and structure. A convolutional neural network (CNN) has been shown to detect cardiac structures that are difficult to evaluate and may prove useful in

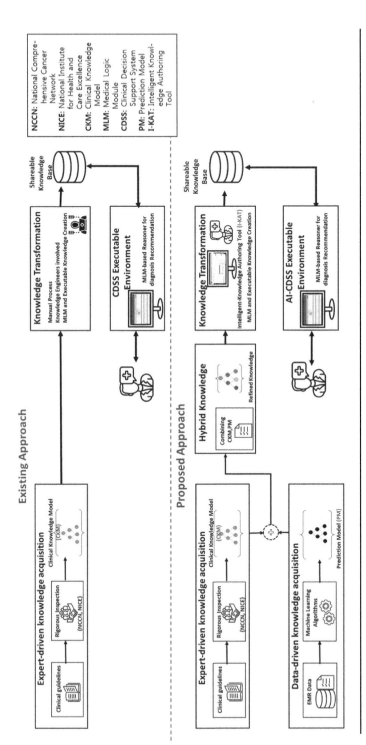

Figure 4.1 Comparison of existing CDSSs and the proposed artificial intelligence-CDSS. CDSS Clinical Decision Support System, CKM clinical knowledge model, I-KAT Intelligent Knowledge Authoring Tool, NCCN National Comprehensive Cancer Network, NICE National Institute for Health and Care Excellence, PM prediction model. (*Source:* Choi D-J, Park JJ, Ali T, Lee, S. Artificial intelligence for the diagnosis of heart failure. *npj Digital Medicine*. 2020;3:54.[5] https://doi.org/10.1038/s41746-020-0261-35; http://creativecommons.org/licenses/by/4.0/)

clinical practice, especially in settings in which there are a limited number of cardiologists qualified to interpret these ultrasound images. Stanford University researchers have trained a CNN on over 2.6 million echocardiogram images from more than 2,800 patients and demonstrated that it is capable of identifying enlarged left atria, left ventricular hypertrophy, and several other abnormalities.[6] The investigation by Ghorbani et al. is noteworthy because it includes such a massive data set, but since it does not include a prospective arm, many cardiologists will likely question its application to bedside care. On a more positive note, however, the researchers have addressed another criticism often aimed at ML-based algorithms: the black box problem.

The black box problem emerges when ML specialists fail to adequately explain the data science behind algorithms. According to *Demystifying Big Data and Machine Learning for Healthcare*, a CNN is "a type of feed-forward artificial neural network in which the connectivity pattern between neurons is inspired by the organization of the animal visual cortex. . . . The model is made of a recursive application of convolution and pooling layers, followed by simple NNs. . . . Pooling layers simply take the output of a convolution layer and reduce its dimensionality."[7] It is likely most clinicians would still find CNNs quite mysterious after reading that explanation. To open up the black box and provide physicians and nurses a good reason to use an ML-enabled algorithm that they can actually comprehend, Ghorbani et al. present readers with "biologically plausible regions of interest" in the echocardiograms they analyze so they can see for themselves the reason for the interpretation that the model has arrived at. For instance, if the CNN says it has identified a structure such as a pacemaker lead, it will highlight the pixels it identifies as the lead. Similar clinician-friendly images are presented for a severely dilated left atrium and for left ventricular hypertrophy.

Early detection of cerebrovascular disorders has likewise attracted the attention of medical informaticists hoping to improve the diagnostic process. Recently, the Centers for Medicare and Medicaid Services (CMS) approved the first technology add-on payment for software designed to help detect stroke. The agency signed off on the new reimbursement decision for Viz.ai's VIZ ContaCT. The manufacturer convinced CMS that its diagnostic aid significantly reduces time to treatment and improves clinical outcomes in stroke patients. Also called Viz LVO, the program uses deep learning to quickly identify suspected large vessel occlusion.

Despite the CMS decision to pay for this service, there is concern among experts in neuroradiology and cardiology about whether the agency has rushed to judgment. The same concern has been voiced among many thought leaders with regard to AI-driven diagnostic and therapeutic tools in general. A recent clinical study found that median time between when a patient arrives at a primary stroke center and when they reach the door at a comprehensive stroke center was reduced by an average of 22.5 minutes—an important achievement since "time equals brain" in this setting. The sooner a CT angiogram can be performed to confirm a blood vessel blockage, the faster life-saving treatment can be administered.[8] But critics question whether the results from the 43 patients enrolled in the trial are generalizable to the general public.

This problem has prompted several stakeholders to call for specific guidelines for conducting studies that evaluate AI-related interventions, and for guidelines on how to report these findings. Similarly, there are behind-the-scenes discussions among academic medical centers, professional associations, vendors, and regulatory agencies to improve the quality of content being input into clinical decision support systems, including content derived from ML studies. Among the groups taking the lead in these efforts: The Standards for Reporting of Diagnosis Accuracy-Artificial Intelligence (STARD-AI) Steering Group, the Consolidated Standards of Reporting Trials (CONSORT-AI) Group, and the Standard Protocol Items: Recommendations for Interventional Trials (SPIRIT-AI) Group.[9] These groups have surfaced to address several vexing issues: Many studies have failed to confirm that their AI-based algorithms remain valid when used on an external validation dataset; they do not always compare their computer-generated outcomes to those generated by their human counterparts; and there are inconsistent definitions of important AI and ML terms, making it difficult to compare the results of several studies. And there are differences in the outcome metrics used, with some trials reporting positive predictive values, others using sensitivity and specificity, and still others relying on AUROC.

To address these shortcomings, the CONSORT-AI and SPIRIT-AI consensus statements spell out several best practices. They both urge researchers to use more precise definitions of key AI terms to eliminate confusion, including class-activation map, input and output data, fine tuning, operational environment, and performance errors.[10,11] The CONSORT-AI Group also emphasizes the need for AI-related trials to include a discussion of generalizability, external validity, and applicability of their findings in a real-world setting. Liu et al. explain: "The measured performance of any AI system may be critically dependent on the nature and quality of the input data . . . A description of the input-data handling, including acquisition, selection and pre-processing before analysis by the AI system, should be provided. Completeness and transparency of this description is integral to the replicability of the intervention beyond the clinical trial in real-world settings."

It is equally important for AI-related investigations to analyze performance errors and how such errors were identified. Because of the nature of many

ML-based algorithms and the complex data science behind them, such errors can be hard to detect. If they go undetected and the algorithms are put into routine clinical use, there can be serious consequences. One problem to be aware of is hidden stratification. A new algorithm may generate impressive results when attempting to detect a certain type of cancer during image analysis. But if the model fails to identify small subsets in the patients being studied—a rare, aggressive cancer, for instance—the consequences can be catastrophic. Clinical trials and retrospective data analyses need to go into enough detail on their performance errors to allow observers to make an informed judgment about the value of the algorithm.[12] The SPIRIT-AI Group discusses similar recommendations in its consensus statement. It too emphasizes the need to recognize the limitations to the generalizability of AI-based algorithms. One obvious example would be an algorithm that requires clinicians to use a specific vendor's devices for implementation of the protocol.

Cancer

Machine learning can play an important role in oncology in two ways: It can be used in the development of neural networks capable of reading pathology or radiology images. And it can be used to analyze text and genomic data to improve diagnosis and prognosis. "Old school" analysis of cancer-related data has relied on interpreting cancer diagnoses, cancer types and tumor grades, as well as the molecular signatures of tumors. But several new sources of data are now available for analysis: whole genome data; single nucleotide polymorphisms; and proteomic and epigenetic data, including the effects of methylation on gene expression. To handle this influx of new information, support vector machines, convolutional neural networks, recurrent neural networks, clustering, and several other digital tools have gained prominence.

One of the most innovative research projects to advance the value of ML in cancer diagnosis was launched by Todd Hollon, with the Department of Neurosurgery, University of Michigan, and associates.[13] They combined a convolutional neural network with simulated Raman histology (SRH), a label-free optical imaging system, to analyze brain biopsy specimens *during* surgery, sending a portion of the specimen to neuropathologists and a portion into the ML-based system. Their conclusion: "In a multicenter, prospective clinical trial ($n = 278$), we demonstrated that CNN-based diagnosis of SRH images was non-inferior to pathologist-based interpretation of conventional histologic images (overall accuracy, 94.6% versus 93.9%)." Not only did their CNN match the performance of human pathologists, it returned results to the surgeon in the operating room to support a brain cancer diagnosis in 2.5 seconds, whereas the conventional technique of sending the specimen to a pathologist required 20 to 30 minutes. Of course, diagnostic protocols are rarely 100% accurate. The combined SRH/CNN arm resulted in 14 errors; the conventional approach that utilized the neuropathologists generated 17 mistakes. The SRH/CNN correctly diagnosed these 17 cases, and the pathologists correctly identified the 14 errors misdiagnosed by the SRH/CNN technique, once again emphasizing the value of combining human and artificial intelligence, rather than relying solely on one or the other. Hollon et al.'s approach also addressed a common criticism of deep learning algorithms, namely, that they rely too heavily on retrospective design.

A great deal of research had been conducted to evaluate the role of ML in breast cancer detection. An international evaluation of 3 deep learning models[14] collected data from over 25,000 British and more than 3,000 American women who had undergone mammography screening, including follow-up data for up to 39 months and confirmation of breast cancer by biopsy—often called "ground truth." Compared to human readers of the imaging, the AI systems generated an absolute reduction in false positives of 5.7% and 1.2% (USA and UK, respectively) and a reduction of 9.4% and 2.7% reduction in false negatives. The researchers also demonstrated cross-validation of the AI models by measuring the performance in the UK data against its performance in the US data. But not testing the system prospectively calls into question its applicability in clinical practice. In real-world settings, there are many other variables to take into account, including the use of different brands of mammography devices. The vast majority of the images analyzed in this study were done on Hologic devices.

The "ground truth" dilemma is another problem faced by many studies that attempt to determine if AI-based algorithms are as accurate as human clinicians in making predictions about cancer. As mentioned above, ground truth refers to the gold standard against which the performance of ML-based algorithms and clinicians are measured. It is assumed that the closer each group comes to matching the conclusions detected by tissue biopsies, the more accurate that group's findings are. But suppose the gold standard is not all that reliable? In many early-stage cancers, pathologists frequently disagree on the interpretation of biopsy findings. It is relatively easy to differentiate between an early stage breast cancer and an invasive cancer, but telling the difference between pre-invasive stages, such as atypia and ductal carcinoma in situ (DCIS), is much more challenging. One study has found that fewer than 50% of pathologists agreed with a panel of experts on the diagnosis of atypia, for instance.[15] Similar disagreements have been documented in the histopathological diagnosis of prostate and thyroid cancer.[16] Such disagreements emerge as a result of the basic difference between a clinical diagnosis and a histopathological diagnosis. An unusual cellular pattern within a tissue specimen may suggest runaway cellular proliferation, but such proliferation does not always result in clinical disease, with all the signs and symptoms that result in a patient's disability and eventual death. In practical terms, such histopathological diagnoses are of very limited value and can result in the overdiagnosis of disease.

Gastroenterology

Several prospective studies have been conducted in this specialty. One of the challenges in making an accurate diagnosis of GI disease is differentiating between disorders that look similar at the cellular level. For example, because environmental enteropathy and celiac disease overlap histopathologically, deep learning algorithms have been designed to analyze biopsy slides to detect the subtle differences between the two conditions. Syed et al.[17] used a combination of convolutional and deconvolutional neural networks in a prospective analysis of over 3,000 biopsy images from 102 children. They were able to tell the differences between environmental enteropathy, celiac disease, and normal controls with an accuracy rating of 93.4%, and a false negative rate of 2/4%. Most of these mistakes occurred when comparing celiac patients to healthy controls. The investigators also identified several biomarkers that may help separate the two GI disorders: interleukin 9, interleukin 6, interleukin 1b, and interferon γ-induced protein 10 were all helpful in making an accurate prediction regarding the correct diagnosis. The potential benefits to this deep learning approach become obvious when one considers the arduous process that patients have to endure to reach a definitive diagnosis of either disorder: Typically, they must undergo 4 to 6 biopsies and may need several endoscopic procedures to sample various sections of the intestinal tract because the disorder may affect only specific areas along the lining and leave other areas intact.

Several randomized controlled trials (RCTs) have been conducted to support the use of ML in gastroenterology. Chinese investigators, working in conjunction with Beth Israel Deaconess Medical Center and Harvard Medical School, tested a CNN to determine if it was capable of improving the detection of precancerous colorectal polyps in real time.[18] The need for a better system of detecting these growths is evident, given the fact that more than 1 in 4 adenomas are missed during coloscopies. To address the problem, Wang et al. randomized over 500 patients to routine colonoscopy and more than 500 to computer-assisted colonoscopies. In the final analysis, the adenoma detection rate (ADR) was higher in the ML-assisted group (29.1% vs. 20.3%, $P < 0.001$). The higher ADR occurred because the algorithm was capable of detecting a greater number of smaller adenomas (185 vs. 102). There were no significant differences in the detection of large polyps.

RCTs have also been performed which have demonstrated that a CNN in combination with deep reinforcement learning (collectively called the WISENSE system) can reduce the number of blind spots during endoscopy intended to evaluate the esophagus, stomach, and duodenum in real time. "A total of 324 patients were recruited and randomised. 153 and 150 patients were analysed in the WISENSE and control group, respectively. Blind spot rate was lower in WISENSE group compared with the control (5.86% vs 22.46%, p<0.001) . . ."[19]

Psychiatry

Machine learning can play a role in the detection and management of psychiatric disorders. For instance, it can be useful in determining which depressed patients are most likely to respond to selective serotonin reuptake inhibitors (SSRIs), addressing a problem facing many patients and clinicians who in the past have had to rely on a long, drawn-out process of trial and error. By using clustering, a form of unsupervised learning, in combination with supervised learning, it is possible to estimate which patients will respond to specific SSRIs. To accomplish this type of modeling and forecasting, traditional depression severity scores need to be linked to well-documented biological markers for depression, including several single nucleotide polymorphisms (SNPs). Clustering, used in conjunction with supervised learning that incorporates genomics data, is capable of separating patient cohorts based on their total symptom severity. Combining both types of data has been shown to predict response to specific SSRIs 8 weeks into a treatment regimen. Athreya et al. used this protocol to evaluate about 1,000 patients with major clinical depression taking citalopram/escitalopram.[20] Using only clinical data in the AI model, the research team predicted patients' response to medication with 60% accuracy. Adding genomic data from 6 SNPs to the analysis improved its predictive ability to 85% in men and 90% in women. They concluded: "We have shown that robust prediction of citalopram/escitalopram treatment outcomes can be achieved in depressed patients by using machine-learning approaches that integrate baseline depression severity with functionally validated pharmacogenomic SNP biomarkers."

Their results also underscore the value of pharmacogenomics and the significant impact it can have on clinical decision making. The 1,030 outpatients in the analysis included those who had been treated in the Mayo Clinic Pharmacogenomics Research Network and the International SSRI Pharmacogenomics Consortium trial. The SNPs that were used to help pinpoint antidepressant responsiveness included variants in *DEFB1, ERICH3, AHR,* and *TSPAN5.*

In vitro studies have associated knockdown of *TSPAN5* and *ERICH3* with decreased serotonin levels; changes in the expression of *DEFB1* and *AHR* have been implicated in the pathophysiology of major depressive disorder. Independent studies demonstrate that such gene/protein relationships are more than just empty correlations. A meta-analysis of 5 randomized clinical trials involving over 1,700 patients with depression has found that patients who received treatment based on pharmacogenomic data were significantly more likely to experience remission, when compared to controls receiving routine care.[21]

The role of pharmacogenomics in patient care extends far beyond clinical depression. Of all the genomics data now emerging, pharmacogenomic data is probably the most immediately useful for clinicians seeking to provide more precise and personalized patient care. Several future-minded clinicians and technologists are already building the infrastructure that will make it a reality at the community level. The goal of that infrastructure is to give clinicians quick access to a patient's gene/drug interactions in the electronic health record (EHR) or through an EHR plug-in that will allow them to adjust medication dosage as needed. R. H. Dolin and associates at Elimu Informatics have produced a prototype for a pharmacogenomics clinical decision support (PGx CDS) service and linked it to an existing commercially available EHR system. The PGx CDS system relies on Fast Healthcare Interoperability Resources (FHIR) and CDS Hooks.[22] The system is triggered when a clinician places a medication order in the EHR. Once that occurs, the system searches for relevant genetic data in a Genomic Archiving and Communication System (GACS) and then notifies the prescribing clinician about any relevant recommendations. If there are no pharmacogenomic test results in the patient's records, the PGx CDS system recommends that a test be ordered when indicated. Dolin et al. state:

> PGx use cases are of particular interest because over half of all primary care patients are exposed to PGx relevant drugs. Studies have found that 7% of U.S. Food and Drug Administration (FDA)-approved medications and 18% of the 4 billion prescriptions written in the United States per year are affected by actionable PGx variants; that nearly all individuals (98%) have at least one known, actionable variant by current Clinical Pharmacogenetics Implementation Consortium (CPIC) guidelines; and that when 12 pharmacogenes with at least one known, actionable, inherited variant are considered, over 97% of the U.S. population has at least one high-risk diplotype with an estimated impact on nearly 75 million prescriptions.[22]

Although third-party payors continue to balk at the idea of reimbursing providers for pharmacogenomic testing, several progressive healthcare systems are pushing the envelope. Mayo Clinic is at the forefront in the effort to bring

PGx testing into mainstream medicine. It has partnered with the Baylor College of Medicine to sequence 77 pharmacogenes from 10,000 patients who are being cared for at the Clinic in Rochester, Minnesota. Some of the results of these tests have been inserted into the Clinic's EHR so that clinicians can act on them.

The EHR already has 19 drug/gene pairs targeted, providing clinicians with decision support alerts, as needed.[23] Richard Weinshilboum, MD, professor of pharmacology and medicine at the Mayo Clinic, believes that within 5 to 10 years, PGx testing will become the standard of care and give clinicians an important tool to let them personalize dosages for each patient. "It sounds like a fairy tale, but it will come," Weinshilboum says. "Eventually, the insurance companies will realize that they're going to ultimately save money over time by virtue of optimizing the drug therapy of the patient."[24]

Predictive analytics is also finding a role in assessing the likelihood that a trauma patient will develop posttraumatic stress disorder (PSTD). As much as 20% of the 30 million patients released from the ED after a trauma event are at risk for a psychiatric disorder, including anxiety, depression, and PTSD.[25] There are documented protocols available to reduce the likelihood of developing PTSD and a few proof-of-concept studies that suggest there are signposts to alert clinicians to the eventual onset of the condition. But with the right combination of routine lab values and psychiatric markers, it is possible to more precisely identify patients most likely to develop PTSD. Among the predictors of the syndrome that have been validated in hundreds of trauma patients in 2 independent prospective studies at Grady Memorial Hospital in Atlanta and Bellevue Hospitals in New York: blood glucose, neutrophils, lymphocytes, creatinine, blood urea nitrogen, anion gap; these biological markers are utilized in combination with 4 key psychiatric markers, as self-reported by patients[25]:

"I felt like I was not there, like I was not part of what was going on."
"I felt confused."
"I get upset when something reminds me of what happened."
"I feel hyper or like I can't stay still."

Katharina Schultebraucks, with the Department of Psychiatry, New York University Grossman School of Medicine, and her colleagues reported: "Across the combined samples, the 12-month prevalence of this provisional PTSD diagnosis was 17.12% (57 of 333). The algorithm predicted provisional PTSD diagnosis at 12 months with high discriminatory accuracy of AUC = 0.87 on the external validation dataset . . . Out of all patients who are predicted to manifest non-remitting PTSD symptoms through 12 months, 90% were presenting such non-remitting symptoms. Only 5% of all patients who were 'resilient' through 12 months were falsely predicted to manifest non-remitting PTSD symptoms."

A similar approach can be used to predict the onset of psychosis. In the past, data from EHRs have been used to help forecast which patients are most likely to develop psychosis but the small number of cases in these studies limit their generalizability. An international team has collected a massive data set (IBM Explorys), which contained standardized, longitudinal, de-identified information on over 100,000 individuals, using a recurrent neural network.[26] Raket et al. divided their data into development and validation data sets, as well as an external validation subset, enabling them to identify a long list of predictors, many of which were unexpected. As expected, there were several psychiatric markers that one might suspect predisposes a person to severe mental illness, including a mental health finding, a drug screening test, diagnosis of a depressive disorder, or bipolar disease. But other predictors included seizures, abnormally lower blood chloride or urea nitrogen in serum or plasma, and a diagnosis of chronic pain. The analysis, which used an ML protocol called DETECT, concluded: "DETECT showed adequate prognostic accuracy to detect individuals at risk of developing a FEP [first episode of psychosis] in primary and secondary care."

When Correlation Implies Causality

Although Raket et al.[26] reported adequate prognostic accuracy and included a very large data set, their conclusion was still based on a retrospective analysis, an observational study design. In other words, they did not establish a cause-and-effect relationship between the predictors they measured and the outcome, namely, the onset of psychosis. Many thought leaders in clinical medicine criticize those in the informatics community for being too quick to use findings like this to justify putting the results into everyday use in patient care. No doubt, prospective studies such as the one conducted by Schultebraucks et al.[25] offer stronger evidential support for using ML-based algorithms in patient care, and, of course, RCTs would be even more assuring.[25] But such criticism is sometimes shortsighted. There are several epidemiological criteria that can help establish causality for observational studies.

Among the epidemiological criteria: (1) The stronger the association between a suspected cause A and its alleged effect B, the greater the likelihood that A does cause B. (2) The sequence of events, that is, its temporality, has a bearing on the relationship of A and B. If one suspects that exposure to an environmental toxin contributes to psychosis, for example, documenting the onset of exposure to the toxin *before* the development of psychosis lends further support to a cause/effect relationship. (3) A dose/response relationship, sometimes referred to as a biological gradient, between a suspected cause and its effect likewise suggests one caused the other. If researchers find that a blood lead level of 10 mcg/dl is associated with mild learning disabilities in children, 15 mcg/dl is linked to moderate deficit, and 20 mcg/dl with severe deficits, this gradient strengthens the argument for causality. (4) A biologically plausible mechanism of action linking cause and effect strengthens the argument. In the case of lead poisoning, there is evidence pointing to neurological damage brought on by oxidative stress and a variety of other biochemical mechanisms. (5) Repeatability of the study findings: If the results of Raket et al. are duplicated by independent investigators, that lends further support to the cause/effect relationship. (6) Biological coherence: The association between cause and effect does not "conflict with known facts about the biology of the disease and how the disease progresses."[27]

The Future Belongs to Advanced Data Analytics

Suggesting that healthcare is entering an era of Big Data and machine learning may imply that good medicine is all about mathematical equations and applying the right statistical model. Nothing could be further from the truth. High-quality patient care remains as much an art as a science. And as in the visual and performing arts, some medical practitioners are more creative, more compassionate, and more skilled than others, and they show more initiative. The key to improving the healthcare ecosystem is giving the best "artists" the best analytic tools. And that's what Big Data and AI-fueled algorithms can accomplish.

Among the healthcare systems at the forefront in this movement is the Mayo Clinic and its recently launched Clinical Data Analytics Platform (CDAP), an AI tool designed to provide insights and encourage discovery. CDAP's initial focus has been on biopharmaceutical insights and knowledge, an initiative that has been launched in conjunction with nference, a Cambridge, Massachusetts-based AI company led by a multidisciplinary team of entrepreneurs from the tech and biotech worlds and PhDs in biology and genomics from MIT and Harvard Medical School. This new initiative explores novel molecular targets, novel pairings of drugs and diseases or indications, identification of subgroups of patients who respond better to a specific medication or family of drugs than the average patient, and automated disease risk and stratification.

Logistically, CDAP includes 3 containers. Container 1 is the algorithm designed to de-identify patient records to be used in the data analysis process; container 2 is the de-identified data itself, and container 3 is the location in which innovative algorithms are used to arrive at insights and knowledge. A more detailed explanation of the data migration plan is illustrated in Figure 4.2.

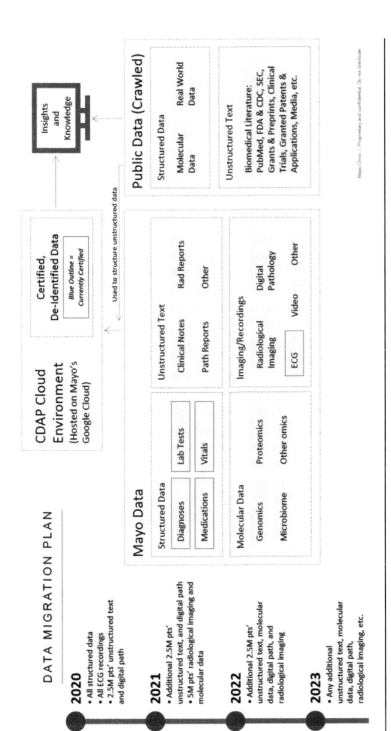

Figure 4.2 The Clinical Data Analytics Platform (CDAP) is an AI tool designed to provide insights and encourage discovery. It taps structured and unstructured data from Mayo Clinic's records, as well as publicly available molecular and real-world data, and unstructured text from the world's biomedical literature. (*Source:* Used with the permission of Mayo Clinic.)

Addressing Criticisms

The list of criticisms surrounding AI and ML is long. As mentioned above, several critics question whether ML-based algorithms are ready for use in routine clinical practice due to a lack of large-scale prospective studies, including RCTs. Others worry that profit motive and overenthusiasm are clouding the judgment of vendors, technologists, and clinicians. Still others remember the failure of early-generation computer-assisted detection systems that were supposed to improve the accuracy of digital screening mammography,[28] and suspect the same of the latest ML algorithms. On the other hand, some stakeholders suspect that AI and ML are being given short shrift by overly conservative clinicians and physician leaders who are comfortable with the status quo and whose reputations have been built on the existing healthcare ecosystem. Similarly, for experienced clinicians to admit that they may need help making difficult diagnostic and treatment decisions from computer-generated clinical decision support systems requires a degree of humility that is lacking among some practitioners.

Although these concerns are difficult to quantify, concerns about biased data sets are not; they can be measured and take various forms, including discrimination based on race, ethnicity, social determinants of health, and geographical location. For instance, researchers have shown that heart disease risk scoring systems give the false impression that Black patients do not require as much care as other patients. There are also algorithms that are less capable of detecting cancer in people of color. To address these and many of ML shortcomings, Owens and Walker recommend algorithm designers become "actively anti-racist."[29] Similarly, evidence suggesting geographical location was documented in an analysis of over 2,600 studies of deep learning. It found that the data sets used to develop ML-based algorithms are disproportionately based on cohorts from California, Massachusetts, and New York. Among the 47 other states, 34 did not contribute a single patient cohort.[30]

Racial and geographic biases are only the tip of the proverbial iceberg. Distributional shift, another potential cause of bias, can occur when an algorithm is trained on data that is somewhat different from the operational data used in patient care. A dataset that taps into all "interesting cases" for instance, may not be a good fit for a more diverse patient cohort from the general public. An algorithm trained on skin cancer cases from a clinic may not accurately detect cancers in office practices in middle class neighborhoods.

In addition to potential bias, other issues that need to be addressed before clinicians can rely on a specific deep learning system include privacy and security, which we discuss in Chapter 7, and the black box problem, mentioned above. Part of the solution to the latter problem is better education. *JAMA* has created excellent audio and video tutorials to explain in plain clinical English how convolutional neural networks work, and in Chapter 5, we explain some of the most common ML tools used in healthcare.

References

1. Forliti M. Platform revolution: curing more people, reaching more lives, anytime, anywhere. Mayo Clinic News Network. July 2, 2020. https://news network.mayoclinic.org/discussion/platform-revolution-curing-more-people -reaching-more-lives-anytime-anywhere/

2. American Diabetes Association. Classification and diagnosis of diabetes: standards of medical care in diabetes 2019. *Diabetes Care.* 2019;42(Suppl. 1):S13–S28. doi .org/10.2337/dc19-S002

3. Cahn A, Shoshan A, Sagiv T, el al. Prediction of progression from pre-diabetes to diabetes: development and validation of a machine learning model. *Diabetes Metab Res Rev.* 2019; e3252. doi.org/10.1002/dmrr.3252

4. De Silva K, Jonsson D, Demmer RT. A combined strategy of feature selection and machine learning to identify predictors of prediabetes. *JAMIA.* 2020;27: 396–406.

5. Choi D-J, Park JJ, Ali T, Lee S. Artificial intelligence for the diagnosis of heart failure. *npj Digital Medicine.* 2020;3:54. doi.org/10.1038/s41746-020-0261-3

6. Ghorbani A, Ouyang D, Abid A, et al. Deep learning interpretation of echo-cardiograms. *npj Digital Medicine.* 2020;3:10. doi.org/10.1038/s41746-019-0216-8

7. Natarajan P, Frenzel J, Smaltz D. *Demystifying Big Data and Machine Learning for Healthcare.* CRC Press/HIMSS; 2017, p. 89.

8. Hassan A, Ringheanu VM, Rabah RR, et al. Early experience utilizing artificial intelligence shows significant reduction in transfer times and length of stay in a hub and spoke model. *Interv Neuroradiol.* August 26, 2020. doi.org/10.1177/15910 19920953055

9. Sounderajah V, Ashrafian H, Aggarwal R, et al. Developing specific reporting guidelines for diagnostic accuracy studies assessing AI interventions: The STARD-AI Steering Group. *Nat Med.* 2020;26:807–812.

10. Rivera SC, Lie X, Chan A-W, et al. Guidelines for clinical trial protocols for interventions involving artificial intelligence: the SPIRIT-AI extension. *Nat Med.* 2020;26:1351–1363.

11. Liu X, Rivera SC, Moher D, et al. Reporting guidelines for clinical trial reports for interventions involving artificial intelligence: the CONSORT-AI extension. *Nat Med.* 2020;26:1364–1374.

12. Oakden-Rayner L, Dunnmon J, Carneiro G, Re C. Hidden stratification causes clinically meaningful failures in machine learning for medical imaging. *ArXiv. org.* November 2019. http://arXiv:1909.12475 **[cs.LG]**

13. Hollon T, Pandian B, Adapa AR, et al. Near real-time intraoperative brain tumor diagnosis using stimulated Raman histology and deep neural networks. *Nat Med.* 2020 Jan;26(1):52–58. doi: 10.1038/s41591-019-0715-9. Epub 2020 Jan 6.

14. McKinney SC, Sieniek M, Godbole V, et al. International evaluation of an AI system for breast cancer screening. *Nature.* 2020;577:89–94.

15. Elmore JG, Longton GM, Carney PA, et al. Diagnostic concordance among pathologists interpreting breast biopsy specimens. *JAMA.* 2015;313(11):1122–1132. doi:10.1001/jama.2015.1405

16. Adamson AS, Welch HG. Machine learning and the cancer-diagnosis problem—no gold standard. *N Engl J Med.* 2019;381:2285–2287.

17. Syed S, Al-Bone M, Khan MN, et al. Assessment of machine learning detection of environmental enteropathy and celiac disease in children. *JAMA Network Open.* 2019;2:e195822.

18. Wang P, Berzin TM, Brown JR, et al. Real-time automatic detection system increases colonoscopic polyp and adenoma detection rates: a prospective randomised controlled study. *Gut.* 2019;68:1813–1819.

19. Wu L, Zhang J, Zhou W, et al. Randomised controlled trial of WISENSE, a real-time quality improving system for monitoring blind spots during esophagogastroduodenoscopy. *Gut.* 2019;68:2161–2169.

20. Athreya A, Neavin D, Carrillo-Roa T, et al. Pharmacogenomics-driven prediction of antidepressant treatment outcomes: a machine-learning approach with multi-trial replication. *Clin Pharmacol Ther.* 2019;106:855–865.

21. Bousman CA, Arandjelovic K, Mancuso SG, et al. Pharmacogenetic tests and depressive symptom remission: a meta-analysis of randomized controlled trials. *Pharmacogenetics.* 2019;20(1):37–47.

22. Dolin RH, Boxwala A, Shalaby J. A pharmacogenomics clinical decision support service based on FHIR and CDS hooks. *Methods Inf Med.* 2018;57:e115–e123.

23. Bielinski S. (n.d.). Pharmacogenomics: right 10K study. Mayo Clinic Center for Individualized Medicine. Retrieved from https://www.mayo.edu/research/centers-programs/center-individualized-medicine/patient-care/clinical-studies/pharmacogenomics-right-10k. Accessed October 10, 2019.

24. Shute D. (n.d.). Pharmacogenomics to eventually touch every patient, everywhere, expert says. Precision Medicine Institute. https://precision-medicine-institute.com/pharmacogenomics-to-eventuallytouch-every-patient-everywhere-expert-says. Accessed October 10, 2019.

25. Schultebraucks K, Shalev AY, Michopoulos V, et al. A validated predictive algorithm of post-traumatic stress course following emergency department admission after a traumatic stressor. *Nat Med.* 2020;26:1084–1088.

26. Raket LL, Jaskolwski J, Kinon BJ, et al. Dynamic ElecTronic hEalth reCord deTection (DETECT) of individuals at risk of a first episode of psychosis: a case-control development and validation study. *Lancet Digital Health.* Published online March 26, 2020. doi.org/10.1016/S2589-7500(20)30024-8

27. Weaver A, Goldberg S. *Clinical Biostatistics and Epidemiology made ridiculously simple™.* Miami, FL: MedMaster Inc.; 2013.

28. Lehman CD, Wellman RD, Buist DS, et al. Diagnostic accuracy of digital screening mammography with and without computer-aided detection. *JAMA.* 2015;175:1828–1837.

29. Owens K, Walker A. Those designing healthcare algorithms must become actively anti-racist. *Nat Med*. 2020;26:1318–1330.
30. Kaushal A, Altman R, Langlotz C. Geographic distribution of US cohorts used to train deep learning algorithms. *JAMA*. 324:1212–1213.

Chapter 5

Exploring the Artificial Intelligence/Machine Learning Toolbox

"It's not magic, it's math." That observation, from Eyal Oren, PhD, at Google Brain, emphasizes a fact many people fail to understand, namely, that the Wizard of Oz behind the curtain is not a wizard at all, but just a gifted mathematician or data scientist. Unfortunately, because brilliant mathematicians and data scientists do not always have the teaching skills to explain how artificial intelligence (AI) and machine learning (ML)–based algorithms work, it's important to draw back the curtain and explain the most common ML tools in plain English. With that mission in mind, we hope to demystify several of these digital tools, including convolutional neural networks, random forest modeling, gradient boosting, clustering, and linear and logistic regression, all of which are used to construct the digital tools that underpin the latest diagnostic and therapeutic innovations. Having a basic understanding of how these tools work should instill more confidence in the clinical recommendations generated by ML-based algorithms—opening up the black box, as it were.

Building on a Firm Foundation

Although convolutional neural networks, random forest modeling, and related technology are the foundation upon which the latest ML-based algorithms are built, to understand these constructs first requires that one be familiar with AI terminology; it likewise requires an awareness that these terms are often defined differently by different experts. The term machine learning itself can be rather "slippery." One reasonably accurate definition is: "Machine learning is an application of artificial intelligence (AI) that provides systems the ability to automatically learn and improve from experience without being explicitly programmed."[1] The term deep learning is a subset of machine learning that corrects its own errors, learning from its mistakes, using layers and backpropagation in an artificial neural network, for instance.

ML is typically divided into 3 categories: supervised learning, which can be subdivided into classification and regression; unsupervised learning; and reinforcement learning. As mentioned above, technologists often explain these terms in ways that make little sense to a person not already familiar with informatics. A Wikipedia entry defines supervised learning this way: "The computer is presented with example inputs and their desired outputs, given by a 'teacher,' and the goal is to learn a general rule that maps inputs to outputs."[2] A better way to understand supervised learning is to work backwards from a desired healthcare goal. Supervised learning has been used effectively in medical image analysis to help differentiate between a melanoma and a normal mole. To create this kind of algorithm, developers start with images that are clearly labeled as either melanoma or normal tissue based a consensus of a panel of expert dermatologists or pathologists—often called ground truth. This approach is referred to as supervised because it starts with the labeled images; unsupervised learning on the other hand starts with unlabeled data; clustering, discussed below, is an example of unsupervised learning.

Once a labeled dataset of images is available, it is usually divided in half, with one half fed into a deep learning system—a convolutional neural network, for instance—that trains it to tell the difference between cancer and non-cancer by pulling out specific features in the images. It may discover that melanomas have irregular edges while moles are round or oval in shape. The system can also recognize other differences, such as the fact that skin cancers are more likely to have uneven coloration, or bleeding. The second half of the dataset would then be used to test the accuracy of the trained model to see how well it can identify the cancer.

The process of reinforcement learning might be compared to the trial and error process that a young child's brain and muscles go though as he or she learns to walk. With each success and failure, the child accumulates new data to help inform the next attempt. The feedback that the brain and muscles receive reinforces the correct set of instructions, as does the "punishment" received from falling on their face with each mistake. Reinforcement learning employs a similar trial and error process to develop an ML-based algorithm; that process relies on a Q-table to know what long-term goal it is supposed to achieve. More details on Q-tables and their role in ML is available in an O'Reilly Media publication.[3]

Artificial Neural Networks

Neural networks are designed to mimic the functioning of the human nervous system, with its neurons and synapses. In a software system, artificial neurons are nodes or layers that are connected to one another, and as each node is excited by data coming from a digital image, that data is sent to the next node. The excitement transferred from one node to the next is represented by a specific number or weight. In the case of the skin cancer algorithm, the excitement is the result of the network analyzing the millions of pixels in each image. The process is explained in plain English in an entertaining video clip from PBS Nova.[4] A deeper exploration of the principles that serve as a foundation for a convolutional neural network, which serve as the basis for the algorithms used to interpret retinal scans to help detect diabetic retinopathy, has been posted online by the *Journal of the American Medical Association*.[5]

Figures 5.1A and 5.1B provide two oversimplified graphics to explain how neural networks function. Data representing the pixels in an image can be sent through nodes in the first input layer, which is then transferred to the next layer, with the strength of each signal indicated by specific numerical values. The goal is to arrive at an output—in this case, a conclusion that the image represents either a melanoma or a normal mole, an example of classification supervised learning. During the initial sweep of each image, the network will make several errors, which are corrected through the process of backpropagation.

Random Forest Modeling

Most clinicians are familiar with decision trees because many diagnostic and treatment decisions rely on such algorithms. Typically, these flow charts include several branches that ask the clinicians to travel down various paths, depending on an assessment of a patient's symptoms or lab results, for example. Following the tree imagery, it takes many branches to make up a decision tree; similarly, it takes several trees to comprise a forest, thus the term random forest modeling (RFM)—a type of machine learning that can be used for both classification and regression analysis.

RFM generates a large series of decision trees and then compares these trees, taking a majority vote to determine which decision makes the most sense. The advantage of RFM over an individual tree is that: "A large number of relatively

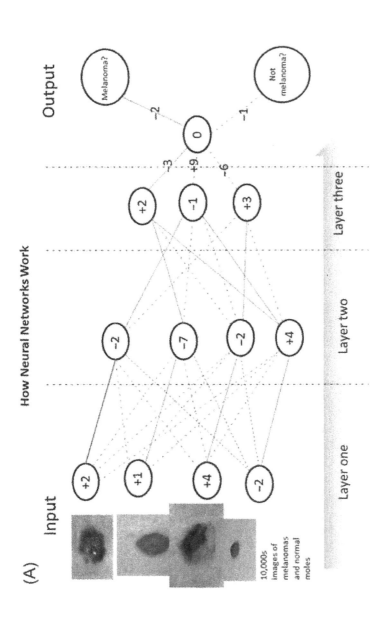

Figure 5.1A A neural network designed to distinguish melanoma from a normal mole will scan tens of thousands of images to teach itself how to recognize small differences between normal and abnormal skin growths. (*Source:* Cerrato P, Halamka J. *The Transformative Power of Mobile Medicine.* Cambridge, MA: Elsevier/Academic Press; 2019:121.[6] Reproduced with permission.)

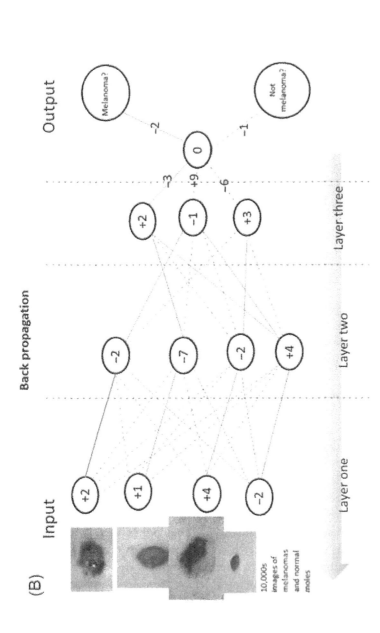

Figure 5.1B During the process of differentiating normal from abnormal tissue, a neural network will make many mistakes. Back-propagation looks back at these mistakes to help the program readjust its algorithms and improve its accuracy. (*Source:* Cerrato P, Halamka J. *The Transformative Power of Mobile Medicine.* Cambridge, MA: Elsevier/Academic Press; 2019:121.[6] Reproduced with permission.)

uncorrelated models (trees) operating as a committee will outperform any of the individual constituent models."[7] Once again, the best way to understand RFM is to work backwards from a healthcare goal. Let's assume that you care for a large population of patients with type 2 diabetes. Most are overweight or, frankly, obese, a major risk factor for the disease, and you want to know how to reduce the likelihood of these patients developing cardiovascular complications. Typically, you might do a literature search on PubMed or consult a clinical decision support system like UpToDate or Clinical Key. If you come across the Look AHEAD trial, a randomized controlled trial (RCT) that evaluated about 5,000 overweight and obese patients, you would find that those on an intensive weight loss and exercise regimen did no better than a control group who only received supportive education.[8] Although the original protocol called for a 13.5-year study, it was terminated after about 9 years because it had no measurable effect on cardiovascular disease or death. Even after conducting a limited sub-group analysis, a forest plot revealed no significant differences.

Experienced clinicians who have cared for diabetics over the years realize that one-size-fits-all treatment does not take into account the heterogenicity in this patient population. Applying RFM to the Look AHEAD trials cohort confirms that. Aaron Baum and his colleagues used RFM and created a series of decision trees (Figure 5.2). The technique randomly splits all the available data—in this case, the stored characteristics of about 5,000 patients in the Look AHEAD study—into two halves. The first half serves as a training dataset to generate hypotheses and construct the decision trees. The second half of the data serves as the testing dataset. As Baum et al. explain, "The method first identifies subgroups with similar treatment effects in the training data, then tests the most promising heterogeneous treatment effect (HTE) hypotheses on the testing data . . ."[9]

Using this technique, Baum et al. constructed a forest that contained 1,000 decision trees and looked at 84 co-variates that may have been influencing patients' response or lack of response to the intensive lifestyle modification program. These variables included a family history of diabetes, muscle cramps in legs and feet, a history of emphysema, kidney disease, amputation, dry skin, loud snoring, marital status, social functioning, hemoglobin A1c, self-reported health, and numerous other characteristics that researchers rarely, if ever, consider when doing a subgroup analysis. The random forest analysis also allowed the investigators to look at how numerous variables *interact* in multiple combinations to impact clinical outcomes.

In the final analysis, Baum et al. discovered that intensive lifestyle modification averted cardiovascular events for two subgroups, patients with HbA1c 6.8% or higher (poorly managed diabetes) and patients with well-controlled diabetes (Hba1c < 6.8%) and good self-reported health. That finding applied to

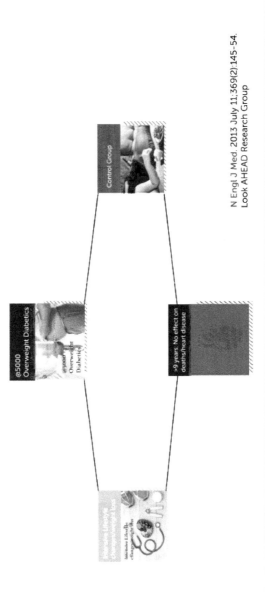

(A)

Look AHEAD trial: Cardiovascular effects of intensive lifestyle intervention in type 2 diabetes

Figure 5.2A The Look AHEAD trial was not able to demonstrate that an intensive diet and exercise regimen reduced cardiovascular complications in diabetes. (Image provided by authors.)

(See Figures 5.2B–5.2D on the following pages.)

N Engl J Med. 2013 July 11:369(2):145–54.
Look AHEAD Research Group

Aaron Baum: Machine learning–based analysis of heterogeneous treatment effects in the Look AHEAD trial

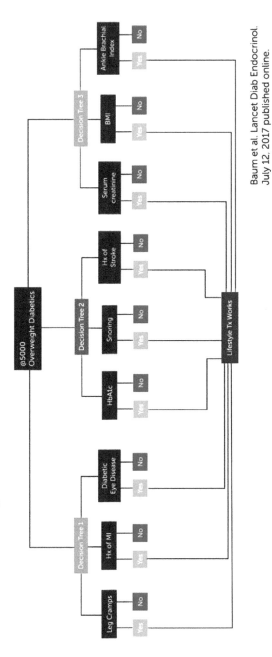

Figure 5.2B Baum et al.[9] reevaluated the Look AHEAD data with a random forest algorithm, breaking up the dataset into 84 subgroups and creating 1,000 decision trees. (Image provided by authors.)

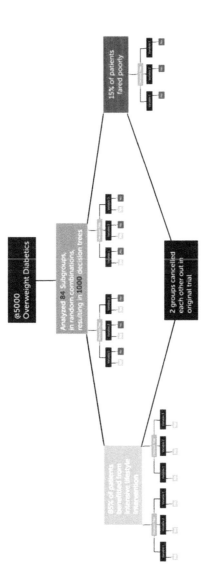

Aaron Baum: Machine learning–based analysis of heterogeneous treatment effects in the Look AHEAD trial

(C)

Baum et al. Diab Endocrinol.
July 12, 2917 published online.

Figure 5.2C The reanalysis revealed that the Look AHEAD study failed to detect differences in outcomes because negative and positive subgroups had cancelled each other out. (Image provided by authors.)

(See Figure 5.2D on the following page.)

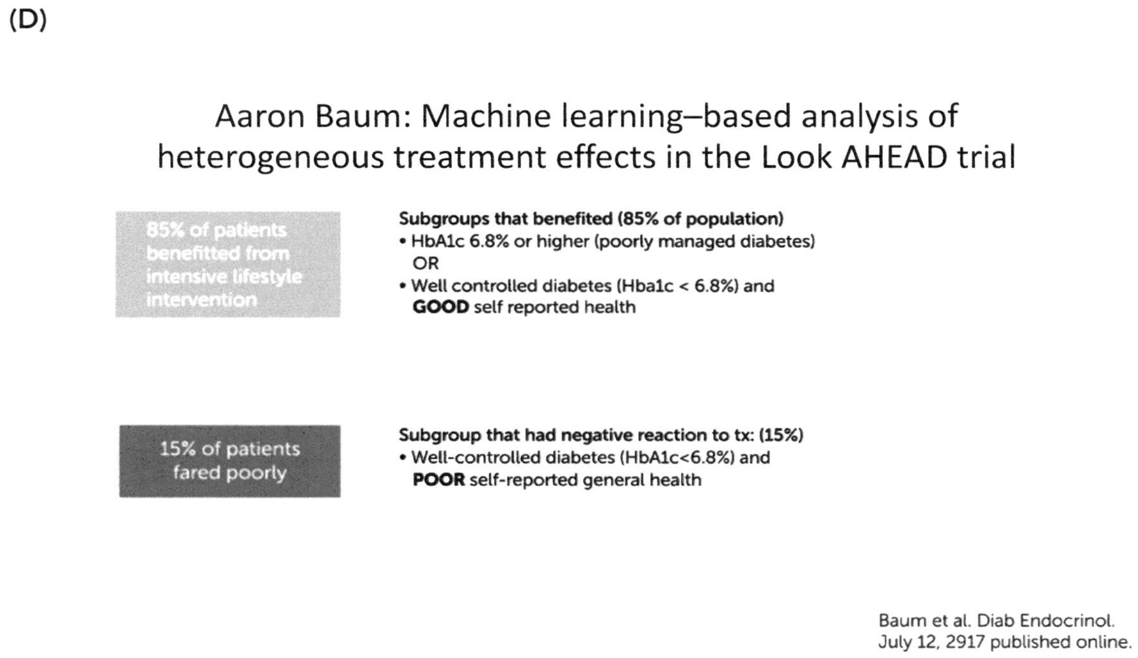

(D)

Aaron Baum: Machine learning–based analysis of heterogeneous treatment effects in the Look AHEAD trial

Subgroups that benefited (85% of population)
- HbA1c 6.8% or higher (poorly managed diabetes)
  OR
- Well controlled diabetes (Hba1c < 6.8%) and **GOOD** self reported health

Subgroup that had negative reaction to tx: (15%)
- Well-controlled diabetes (HbA1c<6.8%) and **POOR** self-reported general health

85% of patients benefitted from intensive lifestyle intervention

15% of patients fared poorly

Baum et al. Diab Endocrinol.
July 12, 2917 published online.

Figure 5.2D Eighty-five percent of patients did benefit from the lifestyle intervention because they fell into 2 unique subgroups; 15% did not because they had different characteristics. (Image provided by authors.)

85% of the entire patient population studied. On the other hand, the remaining 15% who had controlled diabetes but poor self-reported general health responded negatively to the lifestyle modification regimen. The negative and positive responders cancelled each other out in the initial statistical analysis, falsely concluding that lifestyle modification was useless. The Baum et al. reanalysis lends further support to the belief that a one-size-fits-all approach to medicine is inadequate to address all the individualistic responses that patients have to treatment. (A video that explains how RFMs are used in healthcare is available at https://paulcerrato.com/videos/)

Gradient Boosting

Boosting is the operative word in this ML approach because it starts with a weak predictive model and continues to improve its ability to make more accurate predictions by boosting its strength. If, for example, an algorithm is designed to detect skin cancer by analyzing the pixels in a high-resolution image, the goal of gradient boosting is to refine its predictive ability through a series of iterations. If the algorithm only used one feature of a melanoma to determine if a skin lesion is a melanoma—let's say its irregular shape—the algorithm would be a weak classifier. Boosting improves the ability of the algorithm to classify the image as a skin cancer by taking into account many other features, its coloration, bleeding, and so on.

This approach is a type of ensemble learning that uses sequential boosting in which each iteration looks for errors in the algorithm's ability to detect the cancer and distinguish it from a normal mole. To better understand gradient boosting, it helps to contrast it to forms of ensemble modeling that do not take a sequential approach—RFM, for instance. RFM uses a "bagging" approach because it collects data points from the original dataset and generates separate parallel samples chosen at random. Each sample—for example, a collection of skin lesion images—is analyzed separately and then folded into separate models. Then all the models are combined, using a majority voting process or averaging to arrive at the most reliable algorithm. A sequential approach such as boosting starts by extracting data from the original dataset and using the resulting random sample to generate an initial model. Typically, this model will contain numerous errors. Those errors are used to generate a second set of weighted samples to generate a second model that has learned from the observations derived from the first model. The second iteration can then be used to create a third set of weighted samples that is then fed into the next model. Finally, all the models are used to do weighted voting. This weighted voting process results in a more accurate predictive tool.[10]

Traditional boosting techniques, such as adaptive boosting (AdaBoost), use the errors of the current models to assign weights to different training samples for the next iteration, thus putting more emphasis on the model's errors. Gradient boosting, on the other hand, draws inspiration from gradient descent optimization, training the next iteration model to fit to the derivative of the prediction error (also called loss function). Hence, the different weak models form a path in the space of models, each step in an optimized direction toward a more accurate model.[11]

A growing number of data scientists and software developers are favoring gradient boosting—in particular its state-of-the-art version called xgboost—over other ML techniques because it tends to produce more accurate predictions.[12] Gradient boosting is also favored for its ability to handle redundant features without suffering from significant overfitting, and for its handling of missing data, even without imputation. Zhang et al. have compared gradient boosting to artificial neural networks, logistic regression, RFM, and other modeling techniques to estimate that risk of developing type 2 diabetes among more than 14,000 men and 22,000 women in rural China.[13] They found that all the modeling techniques had strong predictive performance, but GBM performed the best with an area under the curve (AUC) of 0.872 when lab data was included in the analysis and 0.817 when it was excluded. The top 10 variables that suggested the likelihood of developing the disease were sweet flavor, urine glucose, age, heart rate, creatinine, waist circumference, uric acid, pulse pressure, insulin, and hypertension for all the techniques evaluated. However, while these 10 predictors were captured by all the models, the relative strengths of each variable differed depending on the technique. For gradient boosting, the "winner" in this analysis, the ranking of important features positioned sweet flavor, age, urine glucose, heart rate, and creatine levels as the strongest predictors. There were also differences in AUC, sensitivity, specificity, and positive predictive values among the various modeling approaches.

Investigators at Oklahoma State University have also tested the relative merits of various modeling techniques in healthcare and likewise found gradient boosting offered an advantage.[14] Extracting patient records from Cerner's electronic health record (EHR) database, they studied 3 prediction models to determine their ability to predict the severity of inflammation among patients with Crohn's disease. Gradient boosting was very accurate (AUC = 0.928). Regularized regression had an AUC of 0.827 and a logistic regression of 0.8274.

Gradient boosting has proven useful in sifting through data on patients with prediabetes to estimate which ones will most likely develop full-blown diabetes. It is difficult to convince many prediabetics to take their condition seriously and make the necessary lifestyle changes to prevent diabetes for 2 reasons: First, they are usually asymptomatic so have no strong incentive to take action. Second, only a small percentage of prediabetics actually convert: 5% to 10% each year.[15] In practical terms, that means convincing apparently healthy persons to make significant changes in their diet and physical activity levels when as many as 9 out of 10 will not develop the disease in any given year. As we discussed in chapter 4, using an AI-enabled assessment tool that takes advantage of gradient boosting can factor in many risk factors not assessed in traditional risk scoring systems by gleaning data from a patient's EHR. More importantly, this type of assessment system can accurately predict which patients will progress to full-blown diabetes, with an AUC of 0.865.[16] The results of this kind of ML-fueled assessment will hopefully carry more weight among prediabetics who are resistant to preventive measures.

This data analysis highlights the ability of big data and advanced AI to generate actionable insights that are impossible to obtain with more traditional statistical analyses or manual evaluation of patient records. As Cahn et al.[16] explain: "Model training was conducted using a rich feature space and a gradient boosted trees classifier using the LightGBM package . . . The model initially included over 900 features, and was trained on 4.9 million time points based upon all individuals who were in the training group. Features included demographic and anthropometric variables, including age, gender, BMI, medication usage, and laboratory results. . . . The individual laboratory tests were used to create multiple variables, including last measured value, maximal and minimal value, slope of change, delta of change, average, and time of last laboratory test recorded."

Clustering

This technique, a form of unsupervised learning, looks at a dataset without labeling its contents. Instead of trying to analyze a collection of medical images or a list of signs and symptoms already labeled as cancer/not cancer, it goes on a "fishing expedition" to look for hidden patterns in the data in the hope of finding new insights or separating a large cohort of patients into subgroups for further analysis. For example, Arjun Arthreya, with the Department of Molecular Pharmacology and Experimental Therapeutics (Mayo Clinic), and associates initially used clustering to study a database of patients with major depressive disorder. Their ultimate goal was to determine if ML-based algorithms that incorporated pharmacogenomic markers and clinical metrics would help determine which antidepressants a patient was most likely to respond to.[17] Clustering revealed 3 subgroups of both men and women based on the Gaussian distribution curves of their symptom severity scores; the scores were collected at 3 separate time points during their course of treatment. Supervised learning techniques were then used to further analyze these clusters, allowing the researchers to identify pharmacogenomic-related single-nucleotide polymorphisms that can guide clinicians in choosing the best antidepressant. Athreya explain: "[T]he patient clusters inferred in this work served as nodes of a probabilistic graph that made it possible to capture the longitudinal variation of depression symptoms over time, conditioned on baseline characteristics and changes in those characteristics at intermediate time points—a process that we have referred to as "symptom dynamics.""[17]

Another example that illustrates the value of cluster analysis addressed a problem that has remained a challenge for diabetes management, namely, the outdated classification for the disease. Currently, it is divided into type 1, type 2, and latent autoimmune diabetes in adults (LADA). One of the weaknesses of the classification system is that it does not let clinicians predict which patients are most likely to require more intensive therapy, which in turn might reduce long-term complications of the disease. Swedish researchers, led by Emma Ahlqvist, used clustering to expand the classification system by identifying 5 groups with very different characteristics and complication risks.[18]

They started with a dataset of nearly 9,000 newly diagnosed diabetics who were part of the Swedish All Diabetics in Scania cohort and concentrated on 6 variables that might suggest the existence of a unique subgroup: glutamate decarboxylase antibodies, age at diagnosis, BMI, HbA1c, insulin resistance, and homeostatic model assessment 2 estimates of β-cell function. The analysis revealed 5 clusters:

Cluster 1: severe autoimmune diabetes (SAID)
Cluster 2: severe insulin-deficient diabetes (SIDD)
Cluster 3 severe insulin-resistant diabetes (SIRD)
Cluster 4 mild obesity-related diabetes (MOD)
Cluster 5: Mild age-related diabetes (MARD)

The clinical implications of this proposed new classification scheme become obvious when one reviews complications associated with these clusters. Ahlqvist et al. explain: "[I]ndividuals in cluster 3 (most resistant to insulin) had significantly higher risk of diabetic kidney disease than individuals in clusters 4 and 5, but had been prescribed similar diabetes treatment. Cluster 2 (insulin deficient) had the highest risk of retinopathy. . . . This new sub-stratification could change the way we think about type 2 diabetes and help to tailor and target early treatment to patients who would benefit most, thereby representing a first step towards precision medicine in diabetes."[18]

The "magic" behind clustering requires that the data be divided into a k number of groups. In k-means clustering, the clusters represent groups that each have similar properties or features. To determine which data points belong in which cluster, a central point is chosen in each proposed grouping and then the rest of the data points are allocated to specific clusters by measuring the distance between each point and the centroid using the formula for Euclidean distance (see Box A):

$$\text{Distance} = \sqrt{\left(x_2 - x_1\right)^2 + \left(y_2 - y_1\right)^2}$$

Box A: How Clustering May Shed Light on Diabetes Classification

To reclassify diabetes into more useful subgroups, it is possible to perform a cluster analysis that looks for hidden patterns in a large database of diabetic patients, using a variety of clinical and laboratory parameters to help focus the analysis. Examples of these parameters were used by Ahlqvist et al.[18] in their cluster analysis and included glutamate decarboxylase antibodies, age at diagnosis, BMI, HbA1c, and homoeostatic model assessment 2 estimates of β-cell function and insulin resistance. (Although the cluster labels in our graphic correspond to three of the clusters identified in Ahlqvist et al., the graphic is not an exact representation of their analysis.)

There are software packages available that allow one to plot each patient in a diabetes dataset on an x-y graph, which in turn can reveal groupings of patients that share many of the same features—features that may be overlooked using more traditional statistical analyses.

Once the data points are input into a scatter plot, the next step is to choose a likely central point for each cluster and then determine which of the nearby patients are part of that cluster. That determination is made by measuring the distance between each patient's data point and the chosen centroid using Euclidean distance:

$$\text{Distance} = \sqrt{\left(x_2 - x_1\right)^2 + \left(y_2 - y_1\right)^2}$$

In this oversimplified cluster analysis, 3 subgroups have been postulated. The analysis has identified a subgroup that is insulin deficient (Cluster 2), one that is severely insulin resistant (Cluster 3), as well as a group with mild obesity-related diabetes (Cluster 4). To determine which data points belong in which cluster, a central point is chosen in each proposed grouping and then the rest of the data points are allocated to specific clusters by measuring the distance between each point and the centroid using the formula for Euclidean distance. In our scatter plot, one such distance measurement is represented by a line drawn between a data point and the orange centroid in Cluster 4. Applying the above equation, the distance between this data point ($x_1 = 3.5$, $y_1 = 2$) and the centroid ($x_2 = 4$, $y_2 = 3$) is 1.8.

Several other mathematical calculations are required to correct errors and the misplacement of data points, moving them from one cluster to another. Since Ahlqvist et al.'s analysis found that patients in several subgroups were treated with similar regimens, despite having different levels of risk and different complication profiles, their clustering suggests the need for a more nuanced classification system than is currently in use.[18]

Linear and Logistic Regression

Although linear and logistic regression are often considered forms of ML, these "old school" tools do not belong in the same category as more recent techniques, which are collectively referred to as deep learning. Nonetheless, they continue to prove invaluable in the development of new research projects and the clinical decision support systems (CDSS) that fuel the digital transformation of healthcare.

The usual tutorials on linear regression are filled with terms such as independent and dependent variables, line slopes, Y intercept, and Pearson coefficients, terms that the average clinician may have learned in school but rarely uses in everyday practice. A more clinician-friendly explanation again works backwards from a real-world example. Suppose you want to determine if there is a connection between dietary intake of sugar and the onset of type 2 diabetes in obese patients who are at risk of the disease because of the excess weight. You might measure the amount of sugar consumed by 100 adults (the independent or explanatory variable), and compare it to the onset of diabetes (the dependent or outcome variable) over a 1-year period. If you create a scatter plot with an X axis for sugar and a Y axis for diabetes onset, it might look like Figure 5.3. Once the data points are inserted in the graph, it is possible to draw a straight line through the data that moves through most of the data points. If the line slants upward from left to right, it indicates a possible association between sugar intake and diabetes, whereas a downward slant indicates a negative correlation. The formula for the regression line is $Y' = a + bx$. In this case, Y' represents the risk of developing diabetes, a is the intercept, that is, the point at which the line cuts across the Y axis; b is the slope of the line, that is, how steep the incline of the line is); and x represents the independent variable, namely, sugar intake.

Whereas linear regression deals with one explanatory variable and one outcome variable, logistic regression is used to make predictions when there is more than one explanatory variable and the outcome is binary in nature, for example, a yes or no outcome. For instance, if one wants to determine risk factors for

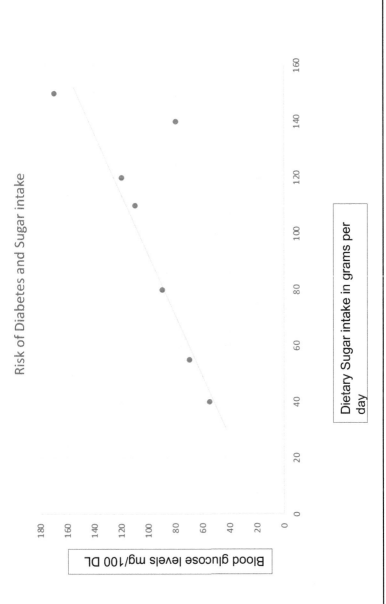

Figure 5.3 In this example of linear regression, a correlation is demonstrated between the amount of dietary sugar that a person consumes and their risk of diabetes. The upward slope of the line indicates a positive association.

developing a stroke (a yes/no outcome), you might track several explanatory variables, including a patient's age, weight, and serum cholesterol levels.

Regression analyses are used in a variety of clinical settings, helping to create numerous diagnostic and treatment models that are used to predict patient outcomes. Plotting the risk of deep vein thrombosis after abdominal surgery, for instance, can help predict which postoperative patients are most likely to develop the complication; certain sets of symptoms and EKG readings experienced by patients who eventually experience a myocardial infarction (MI) can likewise help clinicians predict which patients with chest pain will likely develop an MI.

Of course, anyone who looks at the scatter plot linking sugar with diabetes will immediately realize that there may have been several other variables contributing to the onset of disease, including genetic predisposition. As we discussed in Chapter 4, correlation is not causality. But the strength of a correlation, as indicated by a high correlation coefficient, such as 0.7, lends support to the belief that sugar contributes to diabetes.

Putting AI/ML Tools to Good Use

Several developers are using the ML techniques described above, as well as many others, to create innovative and clinically useful tools that can supplement a physician's or nurse's skills. Diagnostic Robotics, for instance, has been data mining over 19 million articles from the medical literature, in combination with data from EMRs, lab results, sensor readings, time series data, and geospatial patient data, to create an ED triage system that helps predict patients' needs and diagnoses (see Figure 5.4).

To develop the platform for its triage system, Diagnostic Robotics engineers built causal graphs in the spirit of Nordon et al.[19] Construction of these graphs begins with the extraction of predicates from the text of millions of medical studies available in PubMed, with the help of a program called SemRep. "Mediastinal emphysema due to acute bronchial asthma" is one such predicate. The information is then combined with correlations mined from tens of millions of medical records from a variety of EMRs across several countries. Numerous natural language processing (NLP) challenges are raised and overcome by performing latent entities extraction to locate hidden meanings from EMR narrative notes, for example.[20]

Of course, Diagnostic Robotics faces the same objection that many other ML-enhanced diagnostic platforms face, namely, the skepticism of clinicians who do not understand the complex data science and math supporting its conclusions. To address this concern, the triage system provides a clinician-friendly rationale for its conclusions. For example, after analyzing a set of signs and

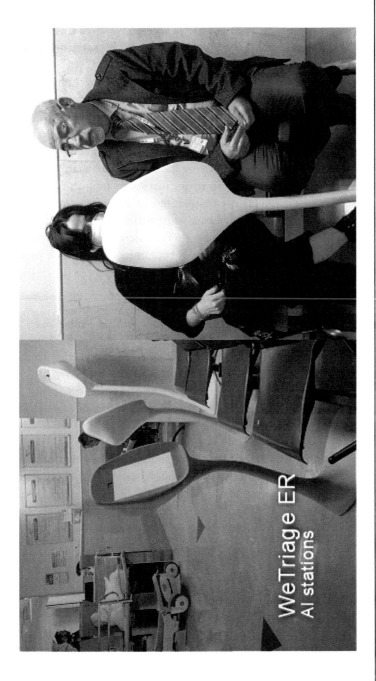

Figure 5.4 Diagnostic Robotics uses data from EMRs, lab results, sensor readings, time series data, and geospatial patient data to create an ED triage system. The patient-facing component of the system is illustrated here. (*Source:* Diagnostic Robotics, used with permission.)

symptoms that suggest sinusitis as the cause, it generates a list of features upon which it bases its recommendation, including the fact that the patient reported a cold or stuffy nose, a headache that got worse when he or she leans forward, and a observation that the headache was not accompanied by vomiting or relief from OTC medication.

Although most ML-based algorithms have focused their attention on diagnosis and treatment of disease, several have concentrated on medication management. MedAware, for instance, uses statistical analysis and neural networks to identify and prevent prescribing errors. Most drug monitoring systems currently in use are rules-based and focus on drug interactions, dosage errors, and allergies. Many clinicians find these tools annoying because they generate alerts that are too obvious or unnecessary, which in turn causes alert fatigue. MedAware uses a data-driven approach and claims a higher rate of error detection. It compares an individual prescription to a database of typical uses of the medication, looking for deviations. The system claims a 10% false alert rate. Support for this big data approach to medication monitoring is contained in a research project reported in the *Joint Commission* journal.[21]

Rozenblum et al. explain:

> *The MedAware system analyzes historical electronic medical records and generates a computational model that captures the population that is likely to be prescribed a given medication and the clinical environment in which the medication is likely to be prescribed. The model identifies prescriptions that are statistically significant outliers given a patient's clinical situation; that is, medications that have rarely or never been prescribed before to similar patients with similar clinical conditions.*

The investigators performed a retrospective analysis, reviewing outpatient data from 2 academic medical centers and generated over 10,000 alerts for the MedAware system. This was compared to a custom-built CDSS developed by Brigham and Women's Hospital and Massachusetts General Hospital. They found that 68.2% of the MedAware alerts would not have been detected by the current CDS system.

Can You Construct Reality by Building Computer Models?

As impressive as many ML-enhanced algorithms are, it is a mistake to think they can replace an experienced clinician's diagnostic and therapeutic skills, or to imagine that they always improve clinical outcomes. Much of the evidence for such algorithms are retrospective analyses and proof-of-concept studies that support the soundness of a constructed model. As Table 5.1 demonstrates, although there are hundreds of published research projects that rely of these two types of evidence, only a small number of reports involve RCTs or other prospective studies.

An exhaustive systematic review and meta-analysis that compared deep learning algorithms to the performance of clinicians has generated mixed results with regard to the ability of ML to interpret medical imaging and provide accurate diagnoses.[22] Liu et al. focused on 82 studies and 142 patient cohorts, concluding: "Our review found the diagnostic performance of deep learning models to be equivalent to that of health-care professionals." Sixty-nine of the 82 studies provided enough detail to extract sensitivity and specificity ratings. Overall, mean sensitivity was 79.1%, and specificity was 88.3%, A closer look at their findings, however, reveal some important caveats. The sensitivity of individual algorithms varied widely, from 9.7% to 100%, whereas specificity ranged from 38.9% to 100%. Only 25 of 82 studies included cross-validation—what the investigators referred to as out-of-sample external validation. In other words, most comparisons of ML-based algorithms to clinicians did not try to determine if their software would work when used in patients outside of their original dataset. If, for example, the program accurately identified pathology in a histology slide among patients in their large academic hospital in San Francisco, it never bothered to determine if it would generate the same accuracy rating among patients in Chicago or elsewhere. Equally troubling was the fact that 72 of the 82 studies analyzed used retrospective data, a less than adequate research protocol that is more likely to miss confounding variables than a prospective study design. Finally, among the 82 studies analyzed, only four allowed clinicians access to additional clinical information; in other words, they could only make their diagnosis based on the medical imaging, which does not mimic what happens in the real world.

If you built model cars or planes as a child, you likely recall the disappointment that came when you realized that they never quite performed as well as the real thing. Perhaps the car doors didn't open, or the wheels didn't spin, or the wings kept falling off the F-15 jet fighter. Many clinicians have faced similar disappointment when they realize that their AI-fueled CDSSs fall far short of expectations.

No one can deny the value of computational models in medicine, but the challenge is to give them the appropriate weight needed to improve clinical decision making, not stifle it. Teufel and Fletcher eloquently summarize this challenge[23]:

Table 5.1 Randomized Controlled Trials and Prospective Studies on Artificial Intelligence (AI) and Machine Learning (ML)

Randomized Controlled Trials

Disease State	Findings	Reference
Colorectal cancer	Colonoscopy combined with deep learning computer-assisted detection improved adenoma detection.	Wang P, et al. *Lancet Gastroenterol Hepatol*. 2020 Apr;5(4): 343–351. https://pubmed.ncbi.nlm.nih.gov/31981517/
Colorectal cancer	Neural network-assisted colonoscopy was more effective than unassisted colonoscopy in detecting adenomas.	Gong D, et al. *Lancet Gastroenterol Hepatol*. 2020 Apr;5(4): 352–361. https://pubmed.ncbi.nlm.nih.gov/31981518/
Upper gastrointestinal disease	Neural network-assisted esophagogastroduodenoscopy reduced blind spot rate.	Wu L, et al. *Gut*. 2019 Dec;68(12):2161–2169. https://pubmed .ncbi.nlm.nih.gov/30858305/
Colorectal cancer	Colonoscopy with AI assistance increased adenoma detection rates, compared to standard colonoscopy.	Wang P, et al. *Gut*. 2019 Oct;68(10):1813–1819. https:// pubmed.ncbi.nlm.nih.gov/30814121/
Childhood cataracts	CC-Cruiser, an artificial intelligence platform, was less accurate in detecting cataracts and making treatment decisions, compared to senior consultants.	Lin H, et al. *EClinical Medicine*. 2019 March 1:52–59. https:// doi.org/10.1016/j.eclinm.2019.03.001

Prospective Studies

Disease State	Findings	Reference
Diabetic retinopathy	Autonomous AI-enhanced algorithm proved effective for detecting mild retinopathy and diabetic macular edema.	Abràmoff M, et al. *NPJ Digit Med*. 2018 Aug 28;1:39. doi: 10.1038/s41746-018-0040-6. eCollection 2018. https:// pubmed.ncbi.nlm.nih.gov/31304320/
Diabetic retinopathy	Automated diabetic retinopathy grading system was at least as effective as manual grading in detecting moderate or worse disease.	Gulshan V, et al. *JAMA Ophthalmol*. 2019 Jun 13. doi: 10.1001/jamaophthalmol.2019.2004. [Epub ahead of print] https://pubmed.ncbi.nlm.nih.gov/31194246/
Diabetic retinopathy	AI-based grading of diabetic retinopathy was used to evaluate 193 patients; it judged 17 as having retinopathy, but only correctly identified 2 patients with true disease, compared to 15 false positive results.	Kanagasingam Y, et al. *JAMA New Open*. 2018 Sep 7;1(5): e182665. doi: 10.1001/jamanetworkopen.2018.2665. https:// www.ncbi.nlm.nih.gov/pmc/articles/PMC6324474/

Congenital cataracts	Convolutional neural network–based algorithm managed diagnosis, risk stratification, and treatment suggestions as accurately as ophthalmologists.	Long E, et al. Nat Biomed Eng. **1**, 0024 (2017). https://doi.org/10.1038/s41551-016-0024
Celiac disease	Trained on duodenal biopsy images, a convolutional neural network was able to differentiate between celiac disease and environmental enteropathy in children.	Syed S, et al. JAMA Open. 2019; 2:e195822. https://jama network.com/journals/jamanetworkopen/fullarticle/2735765
Colorectal cancer	Real-time AI-enhanced ultra-magnifying colonoscopy improves differentiation of small polyps requiring resection from those not requiring resection.	Mori Y, et al. Ann Intern Med. 2018;169:357–366. doi:10.7326 /M18-0249. https://pubmed.ncbi.nlm.nih.gov/30105375/
Nasopharyngeal cancers	Convolutional neural network–based endoscopic imaging outperformed expert oncologists in classifying nasopharyngeal masses as benign or malignant.	Li C, et al. Cancer Commun. 2018;38:1–11. Article no. 59. https://cancercommun.biomedcentral.com/articles/10.1186 /s40880-018-0325-9
Skin cancer	An elementary skin magnifier using polarized light, enhanced with deep learning and sonification algorithms, accurately diagnosed skin cancer.	Dascalu A, et al. EBioMedicine (Lancet). 2019 May 14; 43: 107–113. https://doi.org/10.1016/j.ebiom.2019.04.055
Melanoma	AI-based analysis of dermoscope-derived images demonstrated the ability to diagnose melanoma with accuracy similar to that of specialists.	Phillips M, et al. JAMA Open. 2019;2(10):e1913436. https://doi.org/10.1001/jamanetworkopen.2019.13436
Brain cancer surgery	Convolutional neural network–based algorithm used to analyze intraoperative tissue specimens was non-inferior to pathologists' evaluations.	Hollon, TC, et al. Nat Med. 2020;26:52–58. https://pubmed .ncbi.nlm.nih.gov/31907460/

Source: Halamka J, Cerrato, P. The digital reconstruction of healthcare. N Engl J Medicine Catalyst. 2020 Nov–Dec;1(6). doi.org/10.1056/CAT.20.0082

If successful, [models] allow us to make complex problems more tractable by simplifying them to a set of deep, hidden components that are the main drivers of the visible phenomena the model attempts to explain . . . [A] model must necessarily neglect many aspects of reality to represent adequately the deeper causal structure of that reality. . . . [W]e are forced to make two important assumptions: first, that certain aspects of reality can be ignored because they are irrelevant to the bit of reality that the model attempts to explain; second, that there are parts of the model that 'stand for' things in a way that is meaningful and useful (despite the fact that the model is necessarily an incomplete rendition of reality). Ultimately, therefore, the value of modelling depends upon a clear conceptualization of, and adherence to, the mappings between the model and reality and this, in turn demands a careful consideration of when and where it applies. Incorrect models can be heuristically useful but incorrect application of models will be misleading.

"Misleading" doesn't quite capture the potential harm. When computational models fall short in medicine, the consequences can be devastating, endangering the lives of critically ill patients or missing the diagnosis of a life-threatening medical condition.

Despite our concerns about computational models, we remain optimistic about the future of AI and ML. But as we have stated before, this is evidence-based optimism. A recent partnership between the Mayo Clinic and Google Health is one reason for that optimism. The 2 organizations are using their combined talents to improve radiation therapy for cancer patients.

"During the project's first step . . . Mayo Clinic and Google Health will create and validate an algorithm that can automate healthy tissue and organs from tumors. Developed using de-identified data, the algorithm will boost patient outcomes and reduce the time it takes to plan radiation treatment . . ."[24]

References

1. Expert System Team. What is machine learning? A definition. Expert System. May 6, 2020. https://expertsystem.com/machine-learning-definition
2. Machine learning. Wikipedia. September 26, 2020. https://en.wikipedia.org/wiki/Machine_learning
3. Hu J. Reinforcement learning explained: learning to act based on long-term payoffs. O'Reilly Media. December 8, 2016.
4. PBS Nova. *AI Explained; What Is a Neural Net?* https://www.youtube.com/watch?v=xS2G0oolHpo1358

5. Livingston EH. *Understanding How Machine Learning Works.* Video supplement to: On the prospects for a (deep) learning health care system. *JAMA.* 2018;320:1099–1100. https://edhub.ama-assn.org/jnlearning/video-player/16845576

6. Cerrato P, Halamka J. *The Transformative Power of Mobile Medicine.* Cambridge, MA: Elsevier/Academic Press; 2019.

7. Yiu T. Understanding random forest: how the algorithm works and why it is so effective. *Towards Data Science.* June 12, 2019. https://towardsdatascience.com /understanding-random-forest-58381e0602d2

8. Wing RR, Bolin P, Brancati FL, et al. Look AHEAD Research Group. Cardiovascular effects of intensive lifestyle intervention in type 2 diabetes. *N Engl J Med.* 2013;369:145–154. doi: 10.1056/NEJMoa1212914. https://pubmed.ncbi .nlm.nih.gov/23796131/23796131

9. Baum A, Scarpa J, Bruzelius E, Tamler R, Basu S, Faghmous J. Targeting weight loss interventions to reduce cardiovascular complications of type 2 diabetes: a machine learning-based post-hoc analysis of heterogeneous treatment effects in the Look AHEAD trial. *Lancet Diabetes Endocrinol.* 2017;5:808–815.

10. SAS Tutorial. Gradient boosting explained. February 10, 2020. https://www. youtube.com/watch?v=9wDoiSo8trc. Accessed October 11, 2020.

11. Freund Y, Schapire RE. A decision-theoretic generalization of on-line learning and an application to boosting. *J Comput Syst Sci.* 1997;55:119–139.

12. Chen T, Guestrin C. XGBoost: A scalable tree boosting system. arXiv:1603.02754 **[cs.LG]**. https://arxiv.org/abs/1603.02754

13. Zhang L, Wang Y, Niu M, et al. Machine learning for characterizing risk of type 2 diabetes mellitus in a rural Chinese population: the Henan Rural Cohort Study. *Sci Rep.* 2020;10:4406. doi.org/10.1038/s41598-020-61123-x

14. Reddy BK, Delen D, Agrawal RK. Predicting and explaining inflammation in Crohn's disease patients using predictive analytics methods and electronic medical record data. *Health Informatics J.* 2019;25:1201–1218.

15. Gerstein HC, Santaguida P, Raina P, et al. Annual incidence and relative risk of diabetes in people with various categories of dysglycemia: a systematic overview and meta-analysis of prospective studies. *Diabetes Res Clin Pract.* 2007;78(3):305–312.

16. Cahn A, Shoshan A, Sagiv T, et al. Prediction of progression from pre-diabetes to diabetes: development and validation of a machine learning model. *Diabetes Metab Res Rev.* 2019l e3252.

17. Athreya AP, Neavine D, Carrillo-Roa T, et al. Pharmacogenomics-driven prediction of antidepressant treatment outcomes: a machine-learning approach with multi-trial replication. *Clin Pharmacol Ther.* 2019;106:855–865.

18. Ahlqvist E, Storm P, Karajamaki A, et al. Novel subgroups of adult-onset diabetes and their association with outcomes: a data-driven cluster analysis of six variables. *Lancet Diab Endocrinol.* 2018;6:361–369.

19. Nordon G, Koren G, Shalev V, et al. Building causal graphs from medical literature and electronic medical records. *Proceedings of AAAI Conference on Artificial Intelligence.* 2019;33:1102–1109. doi.org/10.1609/aaai.v33i01.33011102

20. Shoshan E, Radinsky K. Latent entities extraction: how to extract entities that do not appear in the text. *Proceedings of the 2nd Conference on Computational Natural Language Learning.* 2018:200–210. https://pdfs.semanticscholar.org/fd4e /f502932c29477b0b856a054d501b19cbe8c9.pdf?_ga=2.137252528.1020383361 .1603400377-1954216181.1602873509

21. Rozenblum R, Rodriguez-Monguio R, Volk LA, et al. Using a machine learning system to identify and prevent medication prescribing errors: a clinical and cost analysis evaluation. *Jt Comm J Qual Patient Saf.* 2020;46:3–10.

22. Liu X, Faes L, Kale A, et al. A comparison of deep learning performance against health-care professionals in detecting diseases from medical imaging: a systematic review and meta-analysis. *Lancet Digital Health* 2019;1:e271–297.

23. Teufel C, Fletcher PC. The promises and pitfalls of applying computational models to neurological and psychiatric disorders. *Brain.* 2016;139:2600–2608.

24. Horowitz BT. Mayo Clinic, Google announce AI effort to boost radiation therapy for cancer. *Fierce Healthcare.* October 28, 2020. https://www.fiercehealthcare.com /tech/mayo-clinic-google-announce-ai-effort-to-boost-radiation-therapy-for-cancer. Accessed October 28, 2020.

Chapter 6

The Transformative Impact of Conversational Technologies

Developments in artificial intelligence (AI), machine learning (ML), and tele-medicine are no doubt driving the digital reconstruction of healthcare, but innovations in voice technology may outpace all these digital tools as we move deeper into the 21th century's third decade. Some thought leaders in informat-ics refer to it as the "next operating system" and a "fundamental paradigm shift" in the way we communicate and provide healthcare.[1] The evidence does, in fact, suggest that voice and other conversational technologies, which rely heav-ily on AI and ML, are poised to have a transformative impact on the healthcare ecosystem at several levels, including clinical decision support (CDS), direct-to-consumer virtual assistants and chatbots, clinical documentation, and transcrip-tion. All these digital tools and services rest on a foundation of natural language processing (NLP).

Natural Language Processing: Strengths and Weaknesses

At the most basic level, voice technology requires computers to not only recognize human speech but to understand the meaning of words and their relationship to one another in a conversation—no easy task. The existence of so many idioms, colloquialisms, metaphors, and similar expressions makes human language very complex, and more than a little challenging for software programs to decipher. A simple expression from a worried parent, for instance, "My baby is burning up!," can be interpreted in so many ways by a system that looks at the individual words and attempts to understand their relationships in context. The challenge of understanding the meaning of such statements becomes even more daunting when local dialects, accents, and speech impediments are taken into consideration.

To develop a functional NLP system that can interact with patients and clinicians, a lexicon of relevant terms first needs to be created that defines medical terms and the numerous lay expressions that are often used to describe the more technical words. A program capable of performing lexical analysis is also necessary to help interpret the various phrases and combinations of words used during a medical conversation.[2] Finally, the NLP system must be capable of grasping sentence structure, understanding the grammatical rules of each human language it is analyzing, and applying semantic modifiers such as negation and disambiguates.

Although NLP programs remain primitive when compared to the language-processing skills of a 5-year-old child, they are capable of carrying on life-like conversations that enable us to order merchandise, listen to our favorite song, and estimate the risk of COVID-19 infection. Voice technology is also proving useful to clinicians trying to improve their interactions with electronic health record (EHR) systems. In fact, basic math suggests that voice communication should be more efficient than other forms of communication. On average, we speak 110–150 words per minute (wpm), whereas we type only 40 wpm and write only 13 wpm.

A systematic review by informaticists at Vanderbilt University[3] has found several studies that document the ability of computerized speech technology to outperform human transcription, saving on costs and speeding up documentation. Despite such positive reports, these software systems come with their share of problems. Kumah-Crystal et al. sum up the challenges: "The accuracy of modern voice recognition technology has been described as high as 99%. . . . Some reports state that SR [speech recognition] is approaching human recognition . . . However, an important caveat is that human-like understanding of the context (e.g., 'arm' can refer to a weapon or a limb. Humans can easily determine word meaning from the context.) is critical to reducing errors in the final transcription." Inaccuracies in transcription can also occur as a result of speakers hesitating too long, coping with interruptions, and unusual cadences.

These ambient assistants are also being used to speak commands into an EHR system, asking for a patient's latest hemoglobin A1c readings or requesting an e-prescription. They have been used by nursing staff to call up patient allergies as well.

Nuance is one of several companies that have successfully incorporated voice technology into its products. The company is well known for its speech recognition software and recently introduced what it refers to as ambient clinical intelligence (ACI) into its services. ACI allows clinicians to interact with their patients while the software does most of the heavy lifting; it listens to the conversation between physician and patient, automatically writing clinical documentation, including data concerning the history of the present illness, physical exam, assessment, and treatment plan. All the information is then input into the EHR. ACI takes advantage of voice biometrics, ML algorithms, and a 16-microphone–based platform. The company claims that when the patient and clinician speak naturally, it can translate non-clinical terms into clinical terminology and "summarize natural language into coherent sentences."[4]

CDS vendors are also taking advantage of advances in voice technology. UpToDate, for example, has incorporated Nuance's Dragon Medical One into its system. Users can begin a clinical content search with words such as "Hey Dragon, search UpToDate for Type 1 diabetes." If UpToDate users have an Anywhere enterprise license, it is possible to speak commands to obtain medication dosage schedules, drug interactions, clinical calculators, and much more.[5]

Suki, another voice-driven digital assistant designed for clinicians also allows them to speak their notes and orders into an EHR, claiming to reduce documentation time by 76% on average.[6] It can copy notes from previous patient encounters, show the physician or nurse details on a specific patient's medications, and retrieve their vital signs and problem lists. The American Academy of Family Physicians recently tested the platform in its Innovation Laboratory during a pilot project. Their conclusion: "Pilot results were compelling with a 62 percent decrease in documentation time per patient, a 51 percent decrease in documentation time during clinic, and a 70 percent decrease in after-hours charting. Physicians described how the digital assistant allowed them to see their patients and complete their documentation without feeling rushed or having to work after hours. Several physicians described this impact as a "breakthrough" in their practices. Full results and analysis are available in a white paper on the pilot."[7,8]

Using Voice Recognition to Improve the Diagnostic Process

While speech recognition software has taken center stage as a way to improve clinical documentation, the technology is beginning to play an innovative role as a diagnostic aid as well. Analyzing a patient's speech patterns may help reveal patients at risk of coronary heart disease and diagnose congestive heart failure patients who are most likely to require hospitalization. By analyzing voice intensity and frequency, it may be possible to identify patients who are experiencing elevated stress hormone levels, which, in turn, may signal the onset or worsening of heart disease.

With that hypothesis in mind, Elad Maor, MD, PhD, with the Mayo Clinic Department of Cardiovascular Diseases, and colleagues[9] analyzed voice samples from about 100 patients who underwent coronary angiograms for suspected heart disease. They were each asked to contribute 3 voice samples: reading text and describing both a positive and a negative emotional experience into a smartphone. Maor et al. then processed these signals using Mel Frequency Cepstral Coefficients, which is a way to measure subtle variations in voice pitch and intensity. They discovered significant differences in vocal patterns between cardiac patients and normal controls (P = .009 and .04 for positive and negative recordings, respectively). Similarly, they found a significant difference in the intensity of the vocal recordings. Maor et al. theorize: "One possible explanation for our interesting finding is the documented association between mental stress, the adrenergic system, and voice. . . . Emotional stress conditions change the human voice, including an increase in fundamental frequency. . . . [O]ne possible hypothesis to interpret our findings is that the association between voice and atherosclerosis is mediated by hypersensitivity of the adrenergic system to stress. The association between stress, the adrenergic system, and atherosclerosis is well established on the basis of robust data."

There is also evidence to suggest that voice biomarkers may help pinpoint the existence of pulmonary hypertension (see Figures 6.1A and 6.1B).[10] Jaskanwal Deep Singh Sara (also with the Mayo Clinic), in collaboration with scientists from Vocalis Health (an Israeli vendor), used the same voice technology and ML approach discussed in the Maor project to analyze voice recordings of patients enrolled in a study that also evaluated invasive cardiac hemodynamic testing, considered the gold standard for diagnosing pulmonary hypertension. Eighty-three patients each had 3 vocal samples collected though their smartphones and analyzed, using technology that measured pitch, loudness, jitter, and other parameters. Sara et al. explain: "[A] total of 223 acoustic features were extracted from 20 seconds of speech for each patient. The Mel Frequency Cepstral Coefficients were used to extract information from the voice signal, and represent a sound processing tool that is used for voice recognition and for automatic classification between healthy and impaired voices . . . The input for computation of the Mel Frequency Cepstral Coefficients is a speech signal that is further analyzed using the Fourier transform mathematical function. Acoustic features extracted included the following, as previously described: Mel

(A)

Univariate analyses evaluating the association between mean voice biomarker and hemodynamic indices measured in an invasive hemodynamic study.

		Odds Ratio for Association with Voice Biomarker	95% Confidence Interval	P value
Mean Pulmonary Arterial Pressure $\geq$ 35 mmHg	All	1.92	1.00–3.65	0.049*
	PCWP $\geq$ 15mmHg	1.89	0.87–4.12	0.109
	PCWP < 15mmHg	2.09	0.64–6.82	0.223
Pulmonary Vascular Resistance $\geq$ 1.7 Wood Units	All	1.79	0.88–3.65	0.110
	PCWP $\geq$ 15mmHg	2.06	0.81–5.24	0.130
	PCWP < 15mmHg	1.45	0.48–4.43	0.513

Abbreviations–PCWP: pulmonary capillary wedge pressure;
*statistically significant difference between groups.

https://doi.org/10.1371/journal.pone.0231441.t002

Figure 6.1A Sara et al. found their vocal biomarker closely associated with invasive hemodynamic testing of pulmonary arterial pressure, suggesting that it may be useful as a way of diagnosing the condition and monitoring its development.[10]

(See Figure 6.1B on the following page.)

(B)

Multivariable analyses evaluating the association between mean voice biomarker and hemodynamic indices measured in an invasive hemodynamic study.

		Odds Ratio for Association with Voice Biomarker	95% Confidence Interval	P value
Mean Pulmonary Arterial Pressure ≥ 35 mmHg	All	2.31	1.05–5.07	0.038*
	PCWP ≥ 15mmHg	2.72	0.96–7.68	0.060
	PCWP < 15mmHg	2.42	0.62–9.50	0.206
Pulmonary Vascular Resistance ≥ 1.7 Wood Units	All	2.14	0.94–4.87	0.070
	PCWP ≥ 15mmHg	3.86	1.07–13.91	0.039*
	PCWP < 15mmHg	1.66	0.39–7.03	0.493

Abbreviations–PCWP: pulmonary capillary wedge pressure;

* statistically significant difference between groups; † Multivariate analyses adjusted for age, sex, hypertension, diabetes mellitus, and New York Heart Association class.

https://doi.org/10.1371/journal.pone.0231441.t003

Figure 6.1B This graphic presents the results of their multivariable analysis, which took into account several possible confounding variables that may have influenced the results, including patient age, sex, hypertension, diabetes mellitus, pulmonary arterial pressure, pulmonary capillary wedge pressure, right atrial pressure, and cardiac index.[10]

Cepstrum representation, Pitch and Formant Measures, Jitter, Shimmer and Loudness." They found a significant association between an invasively derived hemodynamic index used to measure pulmonary hypertension and the vocal biomarkers. Patients with pulmonary arterial pressure at or above 35 mmHg had higher mean vocal biomarker readings than those with pressure readings at or below 35 mmHg. Given the fact that invasive testing was performed during cardiac catheterization, the non-invasive collection of a patient's voice patterns holds promise. If the findings can be confirmed in controlled clinical trials, it will likely reduce the cost and risk associated with a pulmonary hypertension (PH) diagnosis.

Other investigators have documented similar findings in other specialties. Bonneh et al.[11] have found unique variations in the pitch of children with autism spectrum disorder, with an accuracy of 80%. There also appear to be distinctive vocal patterns among patients with dyslexia, congestive heart failure, Parkinson's disease, and other neurological disorders.[12–14]

Patient-Facing Vocal Technology

While research linking unique voice characteristics to specific disorders suggests such biomarkers may eventually play an important role in patient management, voice technology is already having a significant effect on how consumers and patients obtain self-care and clinician-based care. The public is now using virtual assistants such as Siri, Alexa, and Google Assistant to obtain healthcare information and advice much like the way they used text-based services on websites when the Internet first became popular. For example, Amazon's Alexa has a WebMD skill that provides explanations on the possible causes of chest pain and encourages users to seek medical help if needed. If you directly tell Alexa that you are having chest pain, it urges you to dial 911 or call your emergency contact person. On the other hand, Google Assistant does not respond to "What causes chest pain?" or "I'm having chest pain." It does respond to questions such as "What are the symptoms of a heart attack?" Siri responds to "What causes chest pain?" by linking the user to information from medicinenet.com, which lists some of the common causes. If you tell Siri you are having chest pain, it shows a list of nearby medical centers and a button to call emergency services.

Of course, these examples are only the tip of the iceberg. There are countless questions one can ask voice-activated assistants, as well as several healthcare providers and vendors that are now taking advantage of these tools, with varying degrees of success. The Mayo Clinic has a first-aid Alexa skill and one that provides up-to-date information on COVID-19, as well as a news network. The Cleveland Clinic offers health tips through its Alexa skill. Boston Children's

Hospital likewise has a KidsMD Alexa skill to address parents' questions about children's symptoms.

VisualDx, a CDS company, has a consumer-facing mobile app called Aysa, a symptom checker to help identify common skin conditions that can be accessed with Siri. Similarly, Wolters Kluwer Health has an Alexa skill called Emmi Care Plan that lets clinicians follow up with patients after they leave the hospital. The vendor explains: "Using a natural dialogue that automatically adjusts to patient responses, customers can engage with the skill on Alexa-enabled devices simply by saying, "Alexa, ask Emmi Care Plan" to complete periodic health assessments, reminders and additional education."[15]

The Beth Israel Deaconess Medical Center in Boston has taken advantage of Amazon's virtual assistant by enabling an Alexa skill inside patients' rooms. It lets them ask questions about their room number, who is on their care team, and what their diet prescription is. The skill also allows them to call a nurse, request a social worker, and obtain details on their care plan.[16]

Despite the tremendous potential of patient- and consumer-facing voice technology, there are caveats to keep in mind. When adults are asked to perform health-related tasks using Siri, Alexa, and Google Assistant, the results are sometimes disappointing. Of the 168 voice-activated tasks subjects performed in a recent experiment, 49 (29.2%) could have resulted in harm and 27 (16.1%) in death had they occurred in the real world.[17] Participants were instructed to ask virtual assistants 2 medication-related questions and one emergency-related task. Before participating in the experiment, the 54 subjects were given instructions on how to use each assistant and had time to practice on them before performing the 3 assigned tasks. A closer look at the results provides more insights into how the mistakes developed. The most common problem occurred because participants did not give the assistant enough details to enable it to arrive at the best answer. In the second most common scenario, subjects gave the assistant enough information, but the digital tool responded with partial information.

Fighting Misinformation with Truth and Trust

Unfortunately, experiments like this only tell part of the story. Another reason why so many consumers and patients are misled by ambient assistants and text-based sources is the public's inability to differentiate between reliable sources of medical information and the alternative information sources that rely on hearsay, unfounded conspiracy theories, and the like. The problem is certainly not new. Through the centuries, there have always been charlatans, con men, and uninformed, well-intentioned individuals seeking the public's attention. Although many of their pet theories have faded over time, new ones have filled the void.

A three-pronged approach can help address such misinformation.

Understand the underlying motivation. It is easy to dismiss the public's willingness to believe falsehoods and half-truths, assuming it's a lack of education or gullibility, but the motivation is often more complicated. Research from Aleksandra Cichocka, a political psychologist at the University of Kent in Canterbury, UK, suggests that three psychological needs push people toward conspiracy theories: "the need to understand the world; to feel safe; and to belong and feel good about oneself and one's social groups. . . . Conspiracy beliefs have also been linked to feelings of powerlessness, anxiety, isolation and alienation. Those who feel that they are insignificant cogs in the political machinery tend to assume that there are nefarious influences at play."[18] Steven Pinker, a Harvard University professor of psychology, offers a similar theory. Citing the research of legal scholar Dan Kahan, he points out that: "Certain beliefs become symbols of cultural allegiance. People affirm or deny these beliefs to express not what they *know* but what they *are*. We all identify with particular tribes or subcultures, each of which embraces a creed on what makes for a good life and how society should run its affairs."[19] That observation implies that rejecting a deeply held belief is betraying one's tribe, risking the loss of peer respect.

Accurately report the facts, theories, and controversies when dealing with patients and the general public. This may seem an obvious weapon in the battle to debunk unscientific views, but it can be challenging for several reasons. Explanations take time and most clinicians are too busy discussing diagnosis and treatment in the short window of time they have with each patient to adequately explain the faulty reasoning behind the latest conspiracy about the dangers of the measles vaccine, or the latest theory contending that wearing a mask during a pandemic will cause a toxic buildup of carbon dioxide.

Another barrier to addressing misinformation is the nature of the scientific process itself. During the COVID-19 pandemic, for example, several critics have attacked statements by infectious disease specialists because their advice has changed over time as more data became available from a larger population of infected patients. The assertion, "The experts are constantly contradicting themselves," reflects a lack of understanding of how the scientific method works, as well as the laws of probability. It is a mistake we all fall victim to on occasion. If you bought two Nissan Sentras in recent years and both had serious mechanical problems, it's easy to jump to the conclusion that the model is defective and switch to another brand. But one can only make an informed conclusion about the car based on a much larger sample. A similar process is occurring as more information is collected on the coronavirus. Early theories have had to give way to more nuanced explanations as we gathered more data. That does not invalidate the expertise of infectious disease specialists who have spent their lives studying epidemics. Unfortunately, too few patients and consumers possess the critical thinking skills to appreciate this nuanced approach to arriving at the truth, the kind of Holmesian thinking that requires "mental concentration and weighing every particle of evidence, considering alternative theories, balanced one against the other."[20]

A third obstacle to telling the truth is the fact that we do not always know what the truth *is* on certain health-related issues—and it can be more than a little uncomfortable to admit that. Clinicians have been trained to display confidence in their own pronouncements, and some continue to believe that they are the final authority on all matters medical. That paternalistic approach alienates many patients, especially when they see concrete scientific evidence that contradicts their physician. Now that the public has access to many of the professional resources once reserved for clinicians, this is happening more often. No doubt, years of medical training and experience justify a clinician's self-confidence, but humility and a simple admission of "I don't know" can go a long way toward giving patients confidence in all the other statements we make that are based on stronger evidence.

The value of humility and a willingness to admit the existence of uncertainty was demonstrated by various government officials as they described the dangers of COVID-19 to the public. New Zealand's administration has been praised for the way it discussed the strengths and weaknesses of viral testing, freely admitting on its website that false negative results are a very real possibility. The U.S. Centers for Disease Control and Prevention (CDC) did not mention such uncertainties and has lost some credibility in the eyes of the public as a result.[21]

Build trust with the public. Such humility also builds trust, an essential under-pinning that determines whether patients believe us. In fact, having the public's trust may be even more important than having the truth on one's side, especially in today's world, which is filled with alternative information sources. In 1975, 80% of the American public had "confidence in the medical system" according to Gallup polling. That plummeted to 37% by 2015. Similarly, the General Social Survey found that confidence in medical institutions has been steadily declining from more than 60% in 1974 to 36% in 2016.[22] In an insightful *New England Journal of Medicine* editorial, Richard Baron and Adam Berinsky reflect on this new reality: "Given the decline in trust in the institution of medi-cine, simply asserting medical authority or citing evidence is unlikely to win adherents. Indeed, skepticism regarding facts and expertise is a widespread phe-nomenon today. . . . [U]nder certain circumstances, attempts by experts to cor-rect misinformation may further entrench erroneous beliefs." This skepticism is based in part on the mistaken notion held by many laypersons that everything is subjective, and that science is just another opinion. To effectively mitigate the danger caused by misinformation, Baron and Berinsky recommend recruiting groups and individuals from patients' own peer groups who are willing to speak out against falsehoods because these nonexperts have credibility among members of that peer group. Similarly, finding spokespersons who "speak against their own apparent interest" tends to grab the attention of skeptical individuals. For example, recommendations from the Choosing Wisely campaign, which discouraged physicians from using unnecessary medical tests and procedures, resonated with the public because it played off of the belief among many patients that clinicians order many unnecessary tests because they profit financially. Similarly:

> *In setting the record straight on rumors of "death panels"—false claims that elderly and sick people would be allocated health care on the basis of their supposed value to society—corrections from Republican politicians were more effective than "authoritative" quotes from American Medical Association and AARP experts discrediting the rumor. Similar strategies have proven effective in communication about climate change and about the prevalence of voter fraud.*[22]

Educational initiatives spearheaded by well-liked celebrities can have a similar persuasive effect on public opinion, helping to establish trust. Alan Alda, the actor made famous by *MASH* (the TV series), has been running the Alan Alda Center for Communicating Science at Stonybrook University for several years. His program is helping the public realize that science is not just another opinion, by training scientists to develop better communication skills. He points out that one of the reasons patients and consumers disbelieve experts when they speak is that the experts are so inept at explaining complex issues in plain English.

Finally, when addressing misinformation, it is useful to think of it the same way as addressing many other diseases: An ounce of prevention is worth a pound of cure. Debunking outlandish conspiracy theories and other misinformation is less effective than "prebunking" them. With a little imagination, it is not hard to see what's on the horizon; that, in turn, allows us to warn patients and consumers of these threats to sound reasoning *before* they emerge, while at the same time looking for opportunities to emphasize the benefits of adhering to medical advice that's well supported by evidence.

References

1. Fisher T. The opportunity for voice in healthcare. In: Metcalf D, Fisher T, Pruthi S, Pappas HP, eds. *Voice Technology in Healthcare: Leveraging Voice to Enhance Patient and Provider Experiences.* CRC Press/Taylor & Francis Group; 2020:2–6.

2. Parkhill DE. Managing unstructured data in a health care setting. In: Marconi K, Lehmann H, eds. *Big Data and Health Analytics.* Boca Raton, FL: CRC Press/ Taylor & Francis Group; 2015.

3. Kumah-Crystal YA, Pirtle CJ, Whyte HM, et al. Electronic health record interactions through voice: a review. *Appl Clin Inform.* 2018;9:541–552.

4. Nuance. Witness the exam of the future using ambient clinical intelligence. https://www.nuance.com/healthcare/ambient-clinical-intelligence.html#in-action. Accessed November 17, 2020.

5. Nuance. Clinical content search for Dragon Medical One. https://www.nuance .com/content/dam/nuance/en_us/collateral/healthcare/faq/faq-clinical-content -search-for-dmo-en-us.pdf. Accessed November 17, 2020.

6. Suki. Your digital assistant is here. Meet Suki. https://www.suki.ai. Accessed November 17, 2020.

7. Moriarty M. Suki Clinical digital assistant greatly reduces EHR documentation time and burden for family physicians. American Academy of Family Physicians. June 30, 2020. Accessed November 17, 2020.

8. American Academy of Family Physicians. AAFP innovation lab: reducing documentation burden through the use of a digital assistant. https://www .aafp.org/dam/AAFP/documents/media_center/charts-graphs/digitalassistant -innovationlab--phase-1-whitepaper.pdf. Accessed November 17, 2020.

9. Maor E, Sara JD, Orbelo DM, et al. Voice signal characteristics are independently associated with coronary artery disease. *Mayo Clinic Proceedings.* 2018;93:840–847.

10. Sara JDS, Maor E, Borlaug B, et al. Non-invasive vocal biomarker is associated with pulmonary hypertension. *PLOS ONE.* 15(4):e0231441. doi.org/10.1371/journal .pone.0231441

11. Bonneh YS, Levanon Y, Dean-Pardo O, Lossos L, Adini Y. Abnormal speech spectrum and increased pitch variability in young autistic children. *Front Hum Neurosci.* 2011;4:237.

12. Levanon Y, Lossos-Shifrin L. Method and system for diagnosing pathological phenomenon using a voice signal [Internet]. 2008. Available at http://www .google.com/patents/US739 8213. Accessed September 18, 2016.

13. Ur K, Holi MS. Automatic detection of neurological disordered voices using mel cepstral coefficients and neural networks. In: 2013 IEEE Point-of-Care Healthcare Technologies (PHT). 2013:76–79.

14. Murton OM, Hillman RE, Mehta DD, et al. Acoustic speech analysis of patients with decompensated heart failure: a pilot study. *J Acoust Soc Am.* 2017; 142:EL401–EL407.

15. Wolters Kluwer. Patients recovering at home stay connected to care teams using new Alexa skill, Emmi Care Plan. Nov 17, 2020. https://www.wolterskluwer. com/en/news/patients-stay-connected-using-new-alexa-skill-emmi-care-plan. Accessed November 19, 2020.

16. Cerrato, P, Halamka, J. *The Transformative Power of Mobile Medicine.* Cambridge, MA: Academic Press/Elsevier; 2019:9.

17. Bickmore TW, Trinh H, Olafsson S, et al. Can the use of Siri, Alexa, and Google Assistant for medical information result in patient harm? *J Med Internet Res.* 2018;20:e11510.
18. Cichocka A. To counter conspiracy theories, boost well-being. *Nature.* 2020; 587:177.
19. Pinker S. *Enlightenment Now. The Case for Reason, Science, Humanism and Progress.* New York, NY: Viking; 2018:357.
20. Doyle, AC. *The Hound of the Baskervilles.* In: *The Original Illustrated Sherlock Holmes.* Secaucus, NJ: Castle; 1982.
21. Blastland M, Freeman ALJ, van der Linden S, Marteau M, Spiegelhalter D. Five rules for evidence communication. *Nature.* 2020;587:362–364.
22. Baron RJ, Berinsky AJ. Mistrust in science—a threat to the patient-physician relationship. *N Engl J Med.* 2019;381:182–185.

Chapter 7

Securing the Future of Digital Health

While the digital reconstruction of healthcare is bringing real value to patients and clinicians, it has also brought once unimagined threats to privacy and security, introducing terms our grandparents never heard of. Ransomware and cyberterrorism are constant concerns to healthcare facilities of all sizes, as they are to patients and consumers trying to interact with their providers and with one another. In 2016, we collaborated on a cybersecurity primer titled *Protecting Patient Information*.[1] Although the advice we discussed in that book is still relevant today, cyberattacks have become more sophisticated in the last few years. Staying current on these recent developments is required reading for healthcare executives, technologists, and clinicians.

Investigations into the ransomware threat by the U.S. Federal Government are troubling. In October 2020, The Cybersecurity and Infrastructure Security Agency (CISA), the FBI, and the Department of Health and Human Services (HHS) stated they "have credible information of an increased and imminent cybercrime threat to U.S. hospitals and healthcare providers. CISA, FBI, and HHS are sharing this information to provide a warning to healthcare providers to ensure that they take timely and reasonable precautions to protect their networks from these threats."[2] The most recent alert pointed to two specific threats, the Trickbot trojan and Ryuk ransomware. No doubt these threats have grown because hackers have discovered that hospitals and other healthcare facilities are easy targets and are often willing to pay up to regain access to their data. By one estimate, in 2018, cyberthieves were asking for $5,000 per attack, but that has escalated to $200,000.[3] In one attack, 250 U.S. hospitals and clinics around the country belonging to Universal Health Services were affected by a Ryuk attack. Of course, U.S. healthcare facilities are not alone in this renewed onslaught, one in which patient lives have been jeopardized. The Associated Press, for instance, reported the death of a German patient in urgent need of attention who died because she had to be transported to a second hospital during a cyberattack that affected the first hospital's software system.[4]

Comprehensive Risk Analysis

Ransomware is only one of many threats that require healthcare providers to remain diligent and up to date on the latest hacker tactics and the best preventive measures. Malware can directly infiltrate a medical facility through phishing emails, infecting infusion pumps and other medical devices. It can also reach into a network when employees use public Wi-Fi. Once inside a hospital or medical practice's computer network, cyberthieves may steal sensitive patient data. That includes personal details such as social security numbers and birth dates, and medical data, including their diagnosis and treatment details, as well as Medicare payment details. The stolen data can then be used to impersonate the patient and obtain unauthorized treatment, open new accounts, and much more. Such data breaches are not only dangerous for the patient who has their data compromised; they can also expose the hospital or practice to federal fines for violations of the Health Insurance Portability and Accountability Act (HIPAA) regulations and damage the organization's reputation in the community that it serves, once word gets out about the breach.

One of the first steps to avoid many of these scenarios is a thorough risk analysis to determine where your organization's vulnerabilities are. Unfortunately, many decision makers are still in denial concerning their organization's level of danger and their level of preparedness for an attack, or they are unaware of the value of a comprehensive risk analysis in mitigating the likelihood of an attack. That analysis needs to take into consideration all the devices, software programs, and users who are accessing the facility's network, including anyone allowed to connect their personal equipment. Equally important, the analysis must keep in mind that there are others "looking over your shoulder." Specifically, the HIPAA Security Rule spells out what is expected of a provider in order to demonstrate that it has made a reasonable effort to protect the personal health information it is responsible for. Not meeting that standard can incur financial penalties that may run into the millions of dollars.

"The Security Rule requires appropriate administrative, physical and technical safeguards to ensure the confidentiality, integrity, and security of electronic protected health information" according to the HHS.[5] The Security Rule also requires healthcare providers and their business associates to conduct a risk assessment to make sure that they are complying with said safeguards. Ignoring this mandate can bring penalties through the Office of Civil Rights (OCR).

Fortunately, HHS provides guidelines to help organizations meet the requirements of the Security Rule, which mandates that "[a]ll e-PHI created, received, maintained or transmitted by an organization is subject to the Security Rule."[6] It is important to remember, however, that the government recognizes that healthcare providers only need to implement reasonable and appropriate security measures that are consistent with the size, complexity, and capabilities of their organization. Among the essential questions that your risk analysis needs to address are the following:

- Have you identified the e-PHI (personal health information) within your organization? This includes e-PHI that you create, receive, maintain, or transmit.
- What are the external sources of e-PHI? For example, do vendors or consultants create, receive, maintain, or transmit e-PHI?
- What are the human, natural, and environmental threats to information systems that contain e-PHI?

The results of the risk analysis can then be used to help your organization to:

- design appropriate personnel screening processes;
- identify what data to backup and how;
- decide whether and how to use encryption;
- address what data must be authenticated in particular situations to protect data integrity; and
- determine the appropriate manner of protecting health information transmissions.

The risk analysis also needs to determine the probability, criticality, and impact of potential threats that have been uncovered. HHS explains: "An organization must assess the magnitude of the potential impact resulting from a threat triggering or exploiting a specific vulnerability. An entity may use either a qualitative or quantitative method or a combination of the two methods to measure the impact on the organization."[6] Finally, the entire process requires detailed documentation and periodic review and updates over time. The Security Rule points out that: "A truly integrated risk analysis and management process is performed as new technologies and business operations are planned, thus reducing the effort required to address risks identified after implementation. For example, if the covered entity has experienced a security incident, has had change in ownership, turnover in key staff or management, is planning to incorporate new technology to make operations more efficient, the potential risk should be analyzed to ensure the e-PHI is reasonably and appropriately protected."[6]

The cybersecurity primer we alluded to earlier, *Protecting Patient Information*, outlines some of the assessment toolkits that are available to meet the requirements of the Security Rule, including a useful software program from the Office of the National Coordinator for Health Information Technology called the Security Risk Assessment Tool (SRA Tool).[7]

Preventing Cyberattacks

Even the strongest fortress still has weaknesses, which is why the federal authorities realize that healthcare organizations can only *mitigate* the risk of a cyberattack, not completely eliminate that risk. That said, once you conduct an assessment, it must be followed up with concrete preventive measures, many of which are familiar to most decision makers, including encryption, strong passwords, firewalls, antimalware software, intrusion detection systems, access control protocols, and staff training.

Beyond a doubt, the "carbon-based" units represent the weakest link in any security system. Clinicians, administrators, assistants, and all the other employees working for your organization are the weapons cyberthieves exploit because they continue to be easily tricked into opening emails with infected links or attachments. As Figure 7.1 illustrates, hackers use a variety of tricks to gain employees' trust. They may first study your organization's list of staffers, which is often available on your website, and then try to impersonate someone in authority, or a technician who insists your computer needs to be updated with the latest software. On a more personal level, some thieves appeal to one's ego or interest in the latest fashions or tech toys to lure users to click on an infected link. One of the most deceptive ploys occurs when a hacker sends out thousands of emails claiming to be from your bank or a company you regularly do business with, and, by coincidence, you just got off the phone with the bank or company doing a legitimate transaction. With such close timing, employees often assume the bank or company wants to follow up on the original issue. The list of social engineering tricks used by hackers is almost endless, which is why the best philosophy to teach staff members is as follows: Guilty until proven innocent. Assume every email and text message is an attempt to trick you until

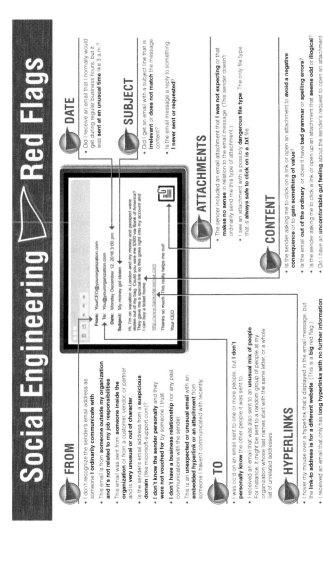

Figure 7.1 Hackers use a variety of tricks to gain employees' trust, often posing as a friend, co-worker, or manager in a phishing email. The goal is to get employees to click on a link or attachment in the message, which in turn downloads malware onto the hospital network. Some clues to help recognize these social engineering tricks are illustrated here. (*Source:* https://blog.knowbe4.com/red-flags-warn-of-social-engineering. Used with permission of the publisher.)

proven otherwise. Any invitation or alleged "urgent" matter alluded to in an email is best investigated by going independently to the original website rather than by clicking on a link or attachments to that website in the suspicious email.

Understanding the Basic Precautionary Steps

Healthcare organizations and their business associates are expected to provide security measures that physically protect their PHI, which includes making sure doors to the servers are secure and a climate control system is in place and working properly, and by ensuring that the only persons given access to the physical space actually need to have access. While those precautions are relatively simple to implement, the electronic safeguards are much more challenging, especially for organizations with a limited budget and/or untrained staffers. The following are among the most important issues to address:

Encryption. Many executives may be surprised, and confused, to learn that HIPAA does not mandate encryption of PHI. In answer to the question: "Is the use of encryption mandatory in the Security Rule?" HHS states: "No. The final Security Rule made the use of encryption an addressable implementation specification. . . . [E]ncryption implementation specification is addressable, and must therefore be implemented if, after a risk assessment, the entity has determined that the specification is a reasonable and appropriate safeguard in its risk management of the confidentiality, integrity and availability of e-PHI. If the entity decides that the addressable implementation specification is not reasonable and appropriate, it must document that determination and implement an equivalent alternative measure, presuming that the alternative is reasonable and appropriate."[8] Although a provider organization may choose to use some other way to protect its PHI besides encryption software, if a tablet or laptop containing such information is lost or stolen and the data is not encrypted, you would have a hard time justifying its lack of encryption.

The type of encryption an organization uses will obviously depend on its financial and manpower resources. Larger hospitals and practices will want to invest in more expensive software systems, but those on very limited budgets and only housing a few personal computers should consider the built-in encryption tools available on Windows and Apple-based machines. Bitlocker is available for certain Windows operating systems, and FileVault can be set up on IOS-based devices. Virtual private networks (VPNs) are likewise an inexpensive way to provide encryption to data being sent back and forth over the Internet.

Firewalls. These hardware and software tools work like the firewall that separates a car's engine from the passenger section. One helpful definition states:

"A firewall is a system that provides network security by filtering incoming and outgoing network traffic based on a set of user-defined rules. In general, the purpose of a firewall is to reduce or eliminate the occurrence of unwanted network communications while allowing all legitimate communication to flow freely. In most server infrastructures, firewalls provide an essential layer of security that, combined with other measures, prevent attackers from accessing your servers in malicious ways."[9] A variety of firewalls are available, including packet filters, stateful inspection firewalls, and application gateways. Details on each type are beyond the scope of this book but are readily available from security vendors and consultants.

Antimalware software. Once upon a time, computer users only needed to worry about viruses, but over the years, several other infectious agents have come upon the scene, making malware a more inclusive term. The term includes viruses, worms, bots/botnets, adware and spyware, ransomware, trojan horses, phishing, and spam. Not to put too blunt an edge on the issue, conducting any type of healthcare business online without a dedicated antimalware system is similar to having unprotected sex—the risks far outweigh the rewards.

When choosing an antimalware vendor, keep in mind the inherent weaknesses of old-school programs. One of the weaknesses of traditional programs is they rely on malware signatures, that is, the "fingerprint" or computer code that identifies a specific piece of malicious software. Unfortunately, there is always a lag between the time a virus goes live and the time an antimalware company is able to create an antidote and distribute it to customers. Some security vendors have taken the next step, using advanced analytics and reputation-based security to spot emerging malware. The latter analyzes billions of files floating around cyberspace to estimate which ones have a good and bad reputation and then blocks suspicious files.

Passwords. Passwords remain an integral part of any privacy and security system, but they are also one of the most abused ingredients in the mix, for several reasons. One of the most vexing issues is creating a password or phrase that is easy for users to remember but difficult enough to fool hackers. No one questions the strength of a password like 3975HFOR-725*924. But the odds of the average human remembering it are nil. The other extreme many choose is equally useless: Choosing a pet name or an easy to guess sequence of numbers. A reasonable middle ground between the 2 extremes can be achieved by choosing a physical location or memorable sentence and then shortening it using initials. For instance, if you frequent a restaurant located near home and you know its address, you might use a password that sums up the sentence: "I eat at 425 Grand Avenue" with a password like IE@425GA. These types of mental tricks help to outsmart the password-cracking programs that are readily available to cyberthieves, which scan millions of common passwords per second. These tools usually include every word in the dictionary, as well as common phrases from popular and classical literature. And in the event that someone does guess your password, or if it is stolen during a separate data breach of your credit agency file, for instance, it makes sense to use two-factor authentication to add stronger protection. For example, one can secure a password on Gmail by following a series of steps that lets you add a smartphone to the security system, in which case you will be required to view a second numerical code that appears on your cell phone and insert that into the Gmail system before you can see your messages. Once that's done, anyone who knows your password will be blocked from gaining access unless they have your cell phone in their possession.

Access Control. Once again, the HIPAA Security Rule provides some guidance on what is expected of healthcare organizations in this regard. Regulation 164.312(a)(1) states in part: "Implement technical policies and procedures for electronic information systems that maintain electronic protected health information to allow access only to those persons or software programs that have been granted access rights. . . ."[10] A three-pronged approach will help meet this requirement: physical, administrative, and technological safeguards. Physical safeguards include locked doors and employee badges; administrative safeguards include a policy and procedures manual that explains which staff members should have access to what kind of data, as well as formal staff training classes. Technological safeguards should block staff members or contractors who do not need to see PHI from getting access to it. Sometimes referred to as role-based access, it would give physicians access to sensitive diagnostic and treatment details but might prevent an accountant from seeing it.

Intrusion Detection and Audit Systems. The purpose of intrusion detection and intrusion prevention hardware and software systems is to monitor and analyze all computer and network activities to look for indications that an unauthorized person has gained access, or that anyone has inserted dangerous code. Once suspicious traffic is detected, it's logged by the program and it alerts the IT administrator of its findings. These systems may be signature-based or anomaly-based; the latter sets up a baseline of normal computer or network activities and then looks for anything outside these norms, labeling it as abnormal and suspicious.

HIPAA regulations require audit controls as well: "Implement hardware, software, and/or procedural mechanisms that record and examine activity in information systems that contain or use electronic protected health information."—Standard: 164.308(a)(1)(ii)(D). For better and worse, electronic patient records and network activities generate mountains of activity logs; many can be useful in tracking unauthorized use of PHI. Firewalls, antimalware programs, servers, and workstations can also provide logs that can be reviewed to look for suspicious activity, unauthorized access, and other types of intelligence to help an organization prevent a data breach or detect it early on. The American Health Information Management Association (AHIMA) offers a helpful primer titled "Security Audits of Electronic Health Information."[11]

Hackers Also Do Their Due Diligence

Reviewing the in-depth research and preparation done by cyberthieves can provide a realistic picture of the relative ease with which they can gain access to a healthcare organization's network. Luis Ayala, a former senior technical expert with the U.S. Department of Defense (DoD), has outlined the 4 steps that hackers often take to infiltrate a hospital's computer network, enabling them to steal patient data, take control of medical devices, and hijack valuable data sources for ransom: footprinting, scanning, enumeration, and network mapping.[12]

Footprinting. In an attempt to promote themselves and give patients access to helpful information, many hospitals and practices have eagerly posted details on the names and contact details on their employees, the type of equipment they use, even where in their facilities that equipment is located. After all, telling the public that they have the latest MRI machine or state-of-the-art digital mammography is a selling point. Unfortunately, ambitious cyberthieves often gather all this publicly available data into their attack portfolio to start the infiltration process. And as Ayala points out, some hackers will even visit a facility to search through dumpsters for clues. If they can discover who makes the medical devices used by a particular hospital, the next step is to obtain user manuals from the manufacturers, which often include the default passwords built into the device. If your organization has not bothered to change that password, you have now given a thief an open invitation.

Another trick used by shrewd hackers is credential harvesting, also called account harvesting, a process in which they can gather vital details about a hospital's network and who maintains it. One source explains: "Account harvesting involves using computer programs to search areas on the Internet in order to gather lists of email addresses from a number of sources, including chat rooms, domain names, instant message users, message boards, news groups, online directories for Web pages, Web pages, and other online destinations."[13]

Scanning. If your facility can be accessed on the Shadon database, a search engine that allows users to look for computers that are connected to the internet, this too can provide an invitation for hackers to retrieve important details on your network, including IP addresses of your devices. This voyeur's dream come true offers free accounts. There are other network-discovery tools, including nMap and Snort, that likewise pose a threat. If these tools reveal some of the software applications being used by a hospital, a hacker's next step is to specifically target these applications to look for weaknesses. Device and software companies typically publish security patches to address these vulnerabilities, but cyberthieves are counting on overworked IT administrators to overlook these patches, or not install them in a timely manner.

Enumeration. At this point in time, if a bad actor has done this much due diligence, they have located a hospital's servers, which operating systems are being used, which applications are running, and much more. The only thing left to do is compile a list of vulnerabilities for all the resources and exploit them. And considering the fact that so many organizations are not up to date on installing security patches, the risk of a data breach is all too real. By one estimate, "there's still over a thousand unpatched devices in the US alone."[14]

One way to take advantage of all the holes in the security net is for the hacker to look for a way to access a hospital network's config.bog file. If they can get in, they can then see passwords and overwrite files and gain root access.

Network Mapping. If a cyberthief has penetrated a computer system to this extent, they can do all sorts of damage. In a nutshell, they are in control and can use phishing scams, man-in-the-middle (MITM) attacks, ransomware, and a variety of other tricks to steal PHI, disrupt everyday clinical and administrative services, and seriously damage your standing in the community. In some cases, they may actually have a more precise map of your hospital network than your IT department!

Beware the Internet of Medical Things

As the above scenario suggests, an organization's medical devices can pose a serious threat to your computer network. But that is only the proverbial tip of the iceberg. The Internet of Things (IoT) includes a long list of mobile devices that have been shown to improve patient monitoring and outcomes but that also open up patients and healthcare systems to data breaches. A growing number of providers are now allowing patients to send data from blood glucose monitors, blood pressure cuffs, bed sensors, and portal EKG devices to their networks. Similarly, clinicians working remotely often use their own laptops, tablets, and smartphones to access a hospital's electronic health record (EHR) system. All these connections are potential opportunities for hackers to infiltrate your computer network.

According to Leon Lerman, CEO and co-founder of Cynerio (a cybersecurity solutions company), most data breaches do not initially begin with a direct attack on a medical device or wearable. In a hospital setting, hackers are more likely to directly attack the network through a phishing scam or other method that allows them to infect the system with malware. But once the infection reaches a device, "that's the biggest impact for the hospital. . . . When an MRI machine is infected by ransomware or a wiper that deletes files, the hospital no longer has an MRI machine working. It's not uncommon for a machine to be down for 4 to 5 days," explained Lerman during an interview. One reason for the easy access to medical devices is the lack of segmentation within the hospital system. In Lerman's experience, the radiology department is probably the most vulnerable because it's hyperconnected, making it more difficult to segment. The second reason radiology is more vulnerable is that the devices use older protocols, such as Digital Imaging and Communications in Medicine (DICOM). Additionally, these machines are easily hacked because they are often running legacy operating systems, including Windows XP and Windows 7, operating systems that are no longer supported by Microsoft, which means there are usually no up-to-date security patches available. Cynerio estimates that about 40% of medical devices are using outdated operating systems.

There are two ways of addressing security issues: Reach out to the manufacturer of the product to ask for an updated OS or security patches when they are available; when that's not possible, isolate the devices from the rest of the hospital network by adhering to well-thought-out segmentation policies. The former solution poses a major obstacle for hospitals and practices because manufacturers do not want outside technicians to touch the product for fear they may disrupt its normal function, which in turn would make the company liable for any patient harm. Fortunately, some of the newer products coming to market are being created with security in mind. They may be accompanied by a Manufacturer Disclosure Statement for Medical Device Security (MDS[2]), which states what security capability the device should have, whether antimalware software has been installed, whether it should be allowed to connect to the Internet, and so on. Network segmentation involves software and hardware solutions that not only isolate network components, including devices, from other parts of the system, but also isolate them from outside communication.

Over time, the digital reconstruction of healthcare will profoundly improve patient care, but this transformation will also require organizations to reexamine their privacy and security systems—and, when necessary, *reconstruct* them to meet the sophisticated threats posed by hackers. This reconstruction may require a significant investment in consultants, new employees, better staff education, and hardware/software upgrades.

References

1. Cerrato P. *Protecting Patient Information: A Decision-Maker's Guide to Risk, Prevention, and Damage Control.* Cambridge, MA: Elsevier/Syngress; 2016.
2. Cybersecurity & Infrastructure Security Agency. Alert (AA20-302A). Ransomware activity targeting the healthcare and public health sector. November 2, 2020. Accessed December 2, 2020.
3. Newman LH. Ransomware hits dozens of hospitals in an unprecedented wave. *Wired.* October 29, 2020. https://www.wired.com/story/ransomware-hospitals -ryuk-trickbot/. Accessed December 2, 2020.
4. Associated Press. German hospital hacked, patient taken to another city dies. *NBC News.* September 17, 2020. Accessed December 2, 2020.
5. HHS.gov. Health information privacy. The Security Rule. Sept 23, 2020. Accessed December 3, 2020.
6. HHS.gov. Final guidance on risk analysis. July 16, 2013. https://www.hhs.gov /hipaa/for-professionals/security/guidance/final-guidance-risk-analysis/index. html. Accessed December 7, 2020.
7. HealthcareIT.gov. Security Risk Assessment tool. September 14, 2020. https:// www.healthit.gov/topic/privacy-security-and-hipaa/security-risk-assessment-tool. Accessed December 7, 2020.
8. HealthcareIT.gov. Health Information Privacy. Is the use of encryption mandatory in the Security Rule? July 23, 2013. https://www.hhs.gov/hipaa/for-professionals/ faq/2001/is-the-use-of-encryption-mandatory-in-the-security-rule/index.html. Accessed January 3, 2021.
9. Anicas M. What is a firewall and how does it work? *DigitalOcean.* August 20, 2015. https://www.digitalocean.com/community/tutorials/what-is-a-firewall-and-how -does-it-work. Accessed January 3, 2021.
10. Cornell Law School Legal Information Institute. 45 CFR § 164.312—Technical safeguards. January 5, 2013. https://www.law.cornell.edu/cfr/text/45/164.312. Accessed January 3, 2021.
11. Walsh T, Miaoulis WM. Privacy and security audits of electronic health information (2014 update). *Journal of AHIMA.* March 2014;85(3):54–59. http://library.ahima .org/PB/PrivacySecurityAudits#.X_N3by1h1hE. Accessed January 4, 2021.
12. Ayala L. *Cybersecurity for Hospitals and Healthcare Facilities.* Fredricksburg, VA: Apress; 2016.
13. Your Dictionary. Account-harvesting meaning. Accessed January 5, 2021.
14. Sussman B. Why won't some organizations patch known vulnerabilities? SecureWorldExpo.com. January 7, 2020. https://www.secureworldexpo.com /industry-news/why-organizations-do-not-patch-security-vulnerabilities. Accessed January 5, 2021.

Chapter 8

The Digital Reconstruction of Global Health

Conversations with governmental health ministers and thought leaders around the world have convinced us that nations large and small are interested in reconstructing their healthcare ecosystem with the help of technology. Many of these nations have launched major digital health initiatives to address seemingly intractable problems, including the urgent need to make patient care more effective, more easily available, and more affordable. Examples of these initiatives are included in Table 8.1. A summary of several projects is provided below.

United Kingdom. The four nations that make up the UK launched NHSX in 2019, a division of the National Health Service (NHS).[1] Scotland has also published its National Digital Health and Care Strategy, identifying several priorities, including the establishment of a joint decision-making board, information governance, strong cybersecurity, and the development of a national digital platform.[2] One of the goals of NHSX is the creation of common technologies and services, including the NHS App. The app includes an online symptom checker and the ability to register and verify one's identity, which, in turn, lets patients book and manage appointments with their personal physician, order repeat prescriptions, and securely view their medical records. The NHS App is now connected to all medical practices in the UK.

Andrew Morris, Chair of Medicine at the University of Edinburgh and Convenor of the UK Health Informatics Research Network, confirmed that

Table 8.1 Digital Transformation Across the Globe

Numerous countries have created strategic plans to develop a wide variety of digital health initiatives. Many of these programs are being spearheaded by governmental bodies and others by non-profit organizations that are partnering with a government's Ministry of Health. The following is only a partial list of the global efforts currently being developed.

Country/Region	Initiative	Resource
China	Ping An Good Doctor, a digital health initiative enrolling over 300 million citizens in an online platform	https://www.linkedin.com/company/ping-an-good-doctor/
Japan	• Millennial Medical Record Project	https://www.dropbox.com/s/vwnz9ypbmvb2kr1/Millennial_Medical_Record_Project%28E%29.pdf?dl=0
	• Introduction of National Medical IDs	
	• Medical Information Database Network (MID-NET) for post-marketing drug safety assessment	https://onlinelibrary.wiley.com/doi/abs/10.1002/pds.4777
Denmark	Danish Digital Health Strategy 2018–2022	https://www.healthcaredenmark.dk/news/danish-digital-health-strategy-2018-2022-now-available-in-english/
Netherlands	The Digital Health market in the Netherlands and Switzerland: opportunities for collaboration in digital health	https://www.rvo.nl/sites/default/files/2019/03/the-digital-health-market-in-the-netherlands-and-switzerland.pdf
	Blockchain for secure patient/provider communication (Mijn Zorg Log)	https://istandaarden.nl/izo/innovaties/blockchain-mijn-zorg-log
	Medmij system to facilitate personal health record system and data exchange	https://www.medmij.nl/en/

Country	Resource	URL
Norway	A Nordic Story about Smart Digital Health	https://norden.diva-portal.org/smash/get/diva2:1297054/FULLTEXT01.pdf
	National Health Archive (NHA) of Norway and Piql	https://www.piql.com/norwegians-digital-health-data-to-be-preserved-for-future-generations/
	Norway's Department of eHealth	https://www.regjeringen.no/en/dep/hod/organisation-and-management-of-the-ministry-of-health-and-care-services/Departments/the-department-of-ehealth/id2473079/
Germany	Digital Health—Germany	https://www.digital-health-germany.org
	Digital Healthcare Act 2019	https://www.bgbl.de/xaver/bgbl/start.xav#__bgbl__%2F%2F%5B%40attr_id%3D%27bgbl119s2562.pdf%27%5D__1584627677728
UK/England	NHSX (National Health Service): Driving forward the digital transformation of health and social care	https://www.nhsx.nhs.uk
UK/Scotland	Scotland's Digital Health and Care Strategy	https://www.gov.scot/publications/scotlands-digital-health-care-strategy-enabling-connecting-empowering/
	Digital Health & Care Institute	https://www.dhi-scotland.com
	eHealth (NHS Scotland)	https://www.ehealth.scot
New Zealand	Ministry of Health Digital Health Strategic Framework	https://www.health.govt.nz/our-work/digital-health
Australia	Australian Digital Health Agency	https://www.digitalhealth.gov.au
	Hospital in the home (health.vic)	https://www2.health.vic.gov.au/hospitals-and-health-services/patient-care/acute-care/hospital-in-the-home
India	India Digital Health Net	https://indiadigitalhealth.net

telemedicine is "part of a portfolio of digital initiatives for the UK, rather than being prioritised above others." He also outlined several challenges that remain to be addressed, including a lack of established standards, earning the public's trust, the lack of open-source code, fragmentation—that is, the lack of a national policy and development of best practices for the NHS—technology, data sharing, and transparency, as well as inadequate interoperability: "We still have a major issue with vendor-lock in and NHS systems cannot talk to one another across the health care system." (Personal communication).

Netherlands. The country has begun focusing on upscaling its digital health programs with a government mandate to exchange medical data among all care providers. That mandate was prompted in part by Babel-like miscommunication that existed among healthcare organizations, many of which used different wording and terminology to discuss the same medical concepts.[3] Bruno Johnannes Bruins, the Dutch Minster for Medical Care, has addressed the challenge, committing more than €400 million to speed up the digital transformation of the country's healthcare ecosystem and speed up information exchange in various sectors. The Dutch government is also investing in blockchain technology to provide its healthcare providers and citizens with a secure digital ledger system that allows them to securely communicate with one another, called Mijn Zorg Log (my care log).

Peter Walgemoed, a Dutch thought leader in digital health, has advocated for the creation of a data-driven health lab co-operative, the goal of which is to build a system that collects medical data of European citizens into a central repository that can be used to organize and curate a vast collection of disconnected information. Sharing this data among healthcare professionals across the European Union can help generate new insights into disease causation and, on a more pragmatic level, can provide more expansive clinical decision support systems (CDSSs) and allow clinicians to have full access to patient records, including genomic, imaging, and laboratory test results, making telemedicine services more effective. Similarly, the Dutch Ministry of Health, Welfare, and Sport and the Ministry of Economic Affairs and Climate Policy, as well as several private organizations, are investing in a personal health record program and telehealth initiatives. Walgemoed states that one of the aims of the GROZ program is that "in 2030, care will be organized 50% more (or more often) in the home environment (instead of in care institutions). . . ." The hospital-at-home movement is also expanding in the Netherlands: "It's a major movement, but still in an experimental/pilot stage. The major University Medical Centers and Teaching Hospitals have programs as well as the industry. . . ." (Personal communication). Successful hospital-at-home programs now exist in England, Canada, Australia, and Israel, as well.[4]

China. The country has undertaken a major digital health initiative, enrolling over 300 million citizens in an online platform called Ping An Good Doctor. It gives 1 in every 3 Chinese Internet users access to medical care, including consultations via their smartphones.[5] This service works with local governments and rural clinics to treat patients virtually and to refer them for in-person medical care when needed. Such telemedicine services are addressing an urgent need in a country that has no formally structured primary care system or well-organized way to connect primary care clinicians to specialists, leading to thousands of patients cramming into waiting areas at China's top hospitals, thus overwhelming medical and nursing staffs (Figure 8.1).

Ben Zhou, MD, president of HAVY International, a consulting firm in Shenzhen, highlighted the problem: "According to the 2017 Future Health Index from Philips, China has the lowest density of skilled health professionals among the 19 countries surveyed (31.5 per 10,000 population),[6] while simultaneously maintaining the highest risk of impoverishing expenditure for surgical care. Separating and directing minor ailments and serious illnesses appropriately into three tiers is critical in reducing waiting times, better utilizing resources available across all of China's medical institutions and addressing the issue of overcrowding in tertiary hospitals. . . . Many see meeting those challenges as a task of utmost priority for the tech industry right now." (Personal communication).

Figure 8.1 China's poorly organized primary care system has resulted in overcrowded waiting areas at many specialty clinics. This image was taken in the dermatology department at a large hospital in Shanghai. (*Source:* John Halamka)

Addressing the Needs of Low-Resource Nations

Whereas China, the UK, and other larger countries have the resources to commit to a national digital health program, low- and middle-income countries (LMICs) struggle to find the capital and workforce to launch such initiatives. Applying relatively inexpensive artificial intelligence (AI) and machine learning (ML)–based systems has the potential to remedy this situation. But for this potential to turn into reality, several obstacles must be overcome. Analysts from the Harvard Global Health Institute point out: "The first relates to the reliability and availability of data. AI systems must be trained using large volumes of data, and the quality of the output reflects the quality of the input. The limited availability or even absence of well-curated, high-fidelity, applicable clinical data sets in LMICs is a foundational challenge."[7] Numerous high-quality datasets have been developed in high-income countries, but there is no guarantee that they apply to the patient populations residing in poorer countries. Unfortunately, validating any ML-based algorithms in these LMICs can be costly. Assuming that these algorithms can be retooled to fit their intended population, the second problem becomes: Will clinicians know how to use them, or even be motivated to try? Finally, most LMICs do not have the regulatory infrastructure to oversee the validation and implementation of said digital tools.

Mehul Mehta, MD, and his colleagues at the Harvard Global Health Institute believe:

> One way forward involves large new investments in data collection, standardization, and availability in resource-poor settings. Though we lack well validated business models for applying AI in LMICs, the marginal cost of electronically deploying AI-based solutions at scale, to augment and enhance the existing health care systems, makes them potentially financially viable. This feasibility is becoming increasingly evident as universal health coverage schemes are implemented and countries scramble for low-cost solutions to augment their health care delivery systems. Fully capturing the economic benefits of AI-driven systems will probably require investments in low-cost technologies such as sensors, phone applications that can capture details of clinical encounters, and public health surveillance data from nontraditional sources.[7]

Another important difference between high-income countries and LMICs that has to be taken into consideration when attempting to use AI and ML is that their basic healthcare needs are quite different. Whereas richer nations must contend with coronary heart disease, cancer, diabetes, and other degenerative diseases, poorer countries have more pressing concerns, including tuberculosis (TB), malaria, dengue, and other infections. AI has been applied to these problems in at least 4 domains: diagnosis, risk assessment, detection of disease outbreaks, and health policy.[8]

ML-based algorithms are now available that can help to automate the diagnosis of pulmonary tuberculosis on thoracic X-rays. One viable approach uses convolutional neural networks (CNNs) trained on the ImageNet dataset to detect plural effusion and an enlarged heart.[9] Similarly, neural networks have been trained to interpret lung ultrasound images to help diagnose pediatric pneumonia, another common problem in LMICs. In one study, a neural network–based algorithm was able to differentiate between normal lungs and the lung infiltrates that characterize pneumonia.[10] The TB and pneumonia algorithms can enhance the diagnostic skills of human clinicians, who are often inadequately trained to detect subtle pathological changes in lung tissue.

Several risk assessment tools are likewise available that take advantage of ML. Researchers from Thailand and the UK have developed a predictive model to help clinicians determine the severity of infection in patients with dengue fever.[11] With the help of a decision tree–based algorithm that incorporates hematocrit, Glasgow Coma score, urinary protein, creatinine, and platelet count, they predicted the severity of patients' conditions with a sensitivity, specificity, and accuracy of 60.5%, 65%, and 64.1%, respectively. Similar risk assessment tools have been developed for malaria and acute pediatric infections.

There's No Stopping the Digital Reconstruction of Healthcare

We began this book with an optimistic point of view by stating that there are rare moments in history when technology, policy, and urgency to change converge. This is one of those moments. Although the COVID-19 pandemic is a global tragedy, it has changed consumer expectations for digital health. We've found that virtual visits, wearable health monitors, and home-based diagnostics work very well. If a suite of services ranging from healthcare maintenance to complex acute care in nontraditional settings meets our needs, why would anyone want to drive an hour, pay $40 for parking, and then sit in a waiting room filled with potentially contagious patients? Of course, there will still be brick-and-mortar facilities for ICU care and surgery, but we're likely to find increasing numbers of services offered remotely. In 2020, the Mayo Clinic's partner Medically Home piloted Home Emergency Department care, followed by Home Hospital admission, followed by Home Post Acute care. Mayo has also piloted hotel-based Post Op Care.

With every passing day, innovators are creating more home-based data sources. We're even seeing the emergence of home-based imaging such as "self-service" ultrasound devices. We're seeing toilet-based urinalysis. We're seeing EEG capabilities embedded in hats. We're only limited by our imagination.

With all these new possibilities, we'll see an increasing need for processing those signals, turning high velocity continuous data into action. AI algorithms will tell us when there is a material change in a patient's condition or a predicted de-compensation. We'll enter a new era of event-driven medicine in which human caregivers are assisted by algorithms which ensure that every professional practices at the top of their license.

As we move forward, we must incorporate solutions that meet each patient at their level of income, technological literacy, and access to connectivity. Reducing disparities and enhancing equity must be the foundation for our work. This may mean that we engineer solutions for low-cost phones or paper-based alternatives, or that may mean we pair patients with a "care navigator" who is delegated to manage their healthcare solutions. With such concerns in mind, the Mayo Clinic has committed $100 million to reducing disparities of care and eradicating racism.

In a time in history where we've seen polarization and increasing social stress, the digital reconstruction of healthcare transcends politics and economics. A connected future that brings safe, quality, and accessible care to all who need it is within our grasp.

References

1. NHSX. Driving forward the digital transformation of health and social care. National Health Service. https://www.nhsx.nhs.uk
2. Scottish Government. Scotland's Digital Health and Care Strategy: enabling connecting connecting and empowering. https://www.gov.scot/publications/scotlands-digital-health-care-strategy-enabling-connecting-empowering/
3. De Korver F. The digital health market in the Netherlands and Switzerland: opportunities for collaboration in digital health. February 2019. https://www.rvo.nl/sites/default/files/2019/03/the-digital-health-market-in-the-netherlands-and-switzerland.pdf
4. Klein S. "Hospital at home" programs improve outcomes, lower costs but face resistance from providers and payers. *The Commonwealth Fund*. https://www.commonwealthfund.org/publications/newsletter-article/hospital-home-programs-improve-outcomes-lower-costs-face-resistance. Accessed January 15, 2020.
5. Cision PR Newswire. Ping An Good Doctor has become the first online healthcare platform with more than 300 million registered users. September 23, 2019. https://www.prnewswire.com/news-releases/ping-an-good-doctor-has-become

-the-first-online-healthcare-platform-with-more-than-300-million-registered
-users-300923026.html. Accessed March 15, 2020.

6. Davenport T, Kalakota R. The potential for artificial intelligence in healthcare. *Future Healthc J.* 2019 Jun;6(2):94–98.

7. Mehta MC, Katz IT, Jha AK. Transforming global health with AI. *N Engl J Med.* 2020;382:791–793.

8. Schwalbe N, Wahl B. Artificial intelligence and the future of global health. *Lancet.* 2020;395:1579–1586.

9. Lopes UK, Valiati JK. Pre-trained convolutional neural networks as feature extractors for tuberculosis detection. *Comput Biol Med.* 2017;89(1):135–143.

10. Correa M, Zimic M, Barrientos F, et al. Automatic classification of pediatric pneumonia based on lung ultrasound pattern recognition. *PLoS ONE.* 2018;13: e0206410. doi: 10.1371/journal.pone.0206410

11. Phakhounthong K, Chaovalit P, Jittamala P, et al. Predicting the severity of dengue fever in children on admission based on clinical features and laboratory indicators: application of classification tree analysis. *BMC Pediatr.* 2019;18:109.

Index